WE WERE NOT ALONE

How an LDS Family Survived
World War II Berlin

Patricia Reece Roper &
Karola Hilbert Reece

DESERET BOOK

Salt Lake City, Utah

Library of Congress Cataloging-in-Publication Data

Roper, Patricia Reece.
    We were not alone : how an LDS family survived World War II Berlin / Patricia Reece Roper, Karola Hilbert Reece.
        p.   cm.
    ISBN 978-1-57008-976-3 (pbk.)
    1. Reece, Karola Hilbert.   2. World War, 1939–1945—Personal narratives, German.
3. Mormons—Germany—Berlin—Biography.   4. Hilbert family—Biography.
5. Berlin (Germany)—Biography.   I. Reece, Karola Hilbert.   II. Title.
    D811.5.R654 2003
    943'.155086'0922—dc21   2003005244

Printed in the United States of America
R. R. Donnelley and Sons

10   9   8   7   6   5   4

CHAPTER 1

It was April of 1938. Of course, I wasn't terribly concerned with the month and year, but what seared itself into my memory was the fact that we were leaving.

I remember that a soft, drizzling rain fell over Leipzig. It made the world outside our window appear mysteriously dark. No children played in the streets that day. Once in a while someone would rush out in the rain with a newspaper or umbrella over his head and hurry off.

From my perch at our apartment window I saw everything that went on in the street, which really wasn't much. My job for the day was to stay out of the way as my older brothers and sisters helped with the packing and moving. My sister Esther and I often sat together and watched the rain. Today, as usual, she was by my side.

The window seat became our refuge and the drizzle a silent friend. Rain droplets gathered in tiny pools on the window until, at last, one drop became too heavy and the pool washed away into a stream, rushing frantically downward. Instead of moving straight down, as I had supposed it would, the stream sometimes traveled so wildly that it lost its course and curved or zigzagged into others before finally colliding with the window frame.

Now, as I think back, I realize how the lives of the people

around me were much like those droplets. So many held to their past until one more change was too much and the strain forced them downward, not straight down but frantically down, without direction, until at last they crashed into the very frame that had held them up.

"Karola, are all your things packed?" Mother's voice startled me. I nodded my head, staring at her. She wasn't like the droplets. She had a course and never faltered from it.

"Mutter, tell me why we're moving again," I said, trying hard not to have an eight-year-old whine in my voice.

"Not again, Karola!" my fifteen-year-old sister Ursula moaned. The broom she held dropped to the floor, and her soft brown curls flapped viciously back when she bent over to retrieve it.

With pleading eyes I looked at Mother.

"Well, all right," she said with a sigh. "I suppose I could use a rest."

I jumped from my seat by the window and bounced on Mother's tender lap. Although I was quite grown up at eight, I still enjoyed that childish luxury. I so loved to gaze into her blue eyes, watch her straight white teeth and loving mouth as she formed words, and rest my head against her chest.

"Five and a half years ago," Mother began, "your father had a very good job here in Leipzig working as a commercial artist. Then when Adolph Hitler came to power, your father was pressured very hard to join the Nazi party."

"Who were the Nazis?" I asked. Even though I thought I knew, I just wanted to make sure I was right.

"People who supported Hitler. Now, try not to interrupt," Mother gently reprimanded. "One day, when the coercion for Father became very intense, he boldly told the Nazi representatives, just like Joshua of old, 'I have chosen whom I will serve, and his name is not Adolph Hitler, but Jesus Christ.'"

A shiver ran down my spine as I pictured Father's tall frame while he firmly stood his ground. My father's steel-blue eyes would have pierced into theirs and his distinguished mustache wouldn't have so much as twitched. This was my favorite part of the story.

"Because of this daring statement, your father lost his job. He couldn't get another because it had to be cleared with the Labor Department in Berlin, and his name was marked. So for the last five and a half years we have had a great struggle to feed you children."

"But it's been a joyful time," I contradicted.

"You didn't have to go to school and try to exchange your hard, dry nut sandwich for someone else's liverwurst," said Edith. I suppose at seventeen, a nut sandwich and made-over, secondhand clothes were not very desirable.

"But we've had so much happiness with the missionaries. When they come to our home I love to hear the stories they tell late into the night."

"Karola, I thought you were asleep," said Mother with mock surprise, her eyes twinkling at me.

"I only pretended to sleep so that you wouldn't make me go to bed," I humbly told her.

"Well, enough," said Mother with a soft chuckle. "Let's finish our packing."

"But you didn't finish the story," I objected, frowning.

"Oh, Karola you know what happened," Horst replied. His hands were full of boxes, so he pushed his glasses up on his nose with his shoulder. Although he was nineteen, I sometimes felt as if he were nine because he teased and tormented me so much. "Father got a job in Berlin and has found an apartment for us to live in. That's why we're packing and you're sitting around asking questions."

"Why don't you and Esther go and look out the window. See if you can see anything," Mother suggested.

"Yes Mutter," I soberly obeyed. I felt this was just an attempt to get me out of the way. It was still raining and nothing interesting was going on.

This dismal moisture had hung over Leipzig for several days now. It made the world outside our window appear tired and depressed.

Since Mother wouldn't continue the story the way I would have liked, I decided to finish it myself with Esther as my audience. Although she was ten, she often listened to me.

"Father has found work in Berlin, so naturally we all have to move. But Arno and Horst will stay here because Arno is going to get married, and Horst has to complete his apprenticeship.

"Father moved two months ago. He wrote and told us he has found an apartment just right for us."

Thump! A dull pain on my head brought me back to the present. I looked up, rubbing the bump that was already forming. "Excuse me, Kaiserlein," said Horst. "It just slipped," he explained, referring to the box he held.

"Mutter!" I cried, bursting into tears, "Horst dropped a box on my head."

"I said excuse me," Horst interjected innocently.

Mother looked at him sternly as she massaged my head.

"Horst what a meanie you are!" Edith fiercely exclaimed.

"She was in the way," Horst said.

I cried louder at this remark.

"How could she be in the way if she's sitting on the window-sill?" asked Edith indignantly.

"That's why I told her to sit there. It's out of the way," Mother added.

"I said I was sorry!"

Mother's lips tightened into a stern line. I could tell that she was suppressing a sermon and using the opportunity to give Horst her well-known, austere stare. I also knew that look, which meant, *behave yourself this instant!* Mother could discipline with only the expression in her eyes.

Just as things began to settle down again, Horst brushed by me and whispered, "Shall I get you an onion so you can cry better?"

Fresh tears started down my cheeks, but Esther brushed them away. "Never mind him. He's just mad because we don't have to help," she explained. "I think he will miss us."

He has a strange way of showing it, I thought, but said nothing.

Everything was packed and ready to go. I felt heavy and excited all at the same time. I was sad at leaving the only home I knew but anxious to explore what laid ahead.

Horst accompanied us to the train station. I looked at the murky walls and felt my gloominess increase. One could tell the floor was black because it was made of asphalt, but the walls, benches, and windows seemed to want to match the floor and were almost as inky. The soot from the coal-operated trains had spared nothing.

Horst told jokes and teased us; and in my childish way I was confused. I thought he might at least show that he felt sad because he had to stay behind.

"Horst, you're always clowning," I chided as he paused in his bantering. "Don't you feel sorry that you won't be coming, too?"

He turned to me and whispered behind his hand, "Don't worry, Karola, I packed plenty of onions for you so that you can cry good. Everyone will feel bad for you. They won't have any time to think about me."

I changed my smile to a pout.

Horst responded with another joke that made me laugh in spite of my efforts to remain solemn.

A noisy crowd of passengers began to board the train. As we stood in line, I looked at Horst. He was smiling, of course, but the sadness in his eyes made me notice how heavy my heart felt. I knew he would miss us terribly, and I would miss him, too, despite his constant teasing ways.

As soon as we boarded the train, my sisters and I ran to the windows to wave good-bye to Horst. He stood on the dark platform smiling and waving. I could still see the broad, black trim on his beige sweater and his brown curly hair being blown back by the windy draft from the train. He wasn't as tall as father, I knew, but seeing him stand alone, bravely waving, added inches to his height I hadn't seen before. I thought I noticed a tear slip down his cheek, but I wasn't sure. I despised the smoky film on the train windows that separated me from my dear Horst.

A slow clang from the train began our journey to Berlin. As the train gradually chugged along faster, picking up speed, Horst remained immobile and got smaller and smaller. I couldn't see the black trim on his sweater, then his head was only a tiny brown dot and finally his beige sweater was too small to be seen.

"Horst," I sobbed, a lump in my throat choking the sound. Edith, Ursula, Esther, and Mother were also crying. Mother put her arms around me and held me closely as the train took us away to Berlin.

※ ※

Berlin was a city with an entirely different pace. Everything was rushed and fast. It seemed the people worried only about getting to their destinations swiftly.

Once Mother stopped a man on a street corner to get directions. She humbly asked, "Excuse me, sir . . . ?"

He immediately cut her off, and replied without even slowing his gait, "I have nothing to excuse you for!"

Mother was perplexed, and we wondered if we could ever grow accustomed to the brisk tempo that was Berlin.

We had been living in Berlin for only a couple of months when one evening, as we sat around the dinner table, the doorbell rang.

"Who could that be?" asked Mother, rising from the table. We all crowded around while Mother opened the door.

There stood Horst, suitcases in hand. His eyes flashed and a smile lit his whole face. "I knew you guys couldn't get along without me!" he said, as he pushed through the door.

My sisters and I rushed towards him, surrounding him with hugs and kisses. He dropped his bags and returned our display of affection, showing his straight white teeth as he laughed. Our gleeful reunion slowly ended and we moved away from Horst, allowing Father a good look at him.

"Horst, what are you doing here?" asked Father. He still seemed stunned at Horst's unexpected arrival.

"I could never get a decent breakfast," he replied.

"What do you mean?" Mother asked, taking his suitcases and setting them in the corner. "Didn't Sister Kuhn feed you well?"

"If I could have eaten her efforts, I would be fatter than a pig. Unfortunately, I couldn't. When she made me a strawberry jam sandwich for breakfast, she would spread on the butter, then lick the knife and dip it into the jam, spread that on the bread and lick the knife absentmindedly. After so much licking, I just didn't have the stomach to eat it anymore."

I burst out laughing and collapsed into a chair. My sisters joined me with giggles, and the tension eased.

"What about your apprenticeship?" Father sternly inquired.

"I thought I would be able to find a good place here to finish it."

"We'll see," said Mother. "At least you could try."

"Then we can all be together again!" Edith happily cried, clapping her hands together.

"Except for Arno," Ursula reminded her.

"Well, when he gets married, Ruth and Arno will live in Leipzig. That'll give us a chance to visit them."

"I guess it's all settled," said Father with a sigh. "Horst, come and have some dinner." He motioned toward an empty chair.

We all sat back down to dinner, laughing and humming because Horst was with us once more.

Father joined in the laughter for a while, then became very serious. It took a few moments for me to notice his solemn expression between my giggles, but when I saw him, I swallowed my next laugh and looked from him to Mother.

"What is it, Paul?" Mother asked him.

"I've been waiting for the opportunity to talk to all of you," he said. My brothers and sisters erased the smiles from their faces and looked at each other.

Father waited until the silence in the room crept around us, sending a shiver down my spine. I was amazed at the contrast in the atmosphere. One moment I was happy and laughing, the next moment my ears rang with the solemn low note of quiet.

Now the room was engulfed in a complete hush, Father cleared his throat and began, "When I was still looking for an apartment for the rest of you, I clipped three advertisements from the paper and put them in my wallet. On a Saturday evening, I went to a public swimming pool to relax before looking them up."

"You mean to bathe, don't you?" asked Horst with a grin. The silence in the room shattered like a broken vase as my sisters and I burst into laughter.

Father stared at Horst and was just about to speak when Mother said, "He means what he says, Horst."

"Oh," Horst innocently replied. "I just thought that since his apartment didn't have a tub, he would have gone swimming so he could smell his best before investigating apartments."

I had to concentrate feverishly on the broad, gold border of my plate to keep from laughing hysterically. If Horst discovered my predicament, his tormenting would surely increase.

Not a single snicker escaped our lips, and after a seemingly eternal silence, Father proceeded. "I watched the lifeguard and decided to approach him to ask about the addresses."

"Why?" I asked. "Couldn't you find them?"

"No, as you know, in Berlin the streets go by name only. They also begin numbering the buildings on one side of the street and continue until the street ends. Then, they simply jump across the street and start numbering again. It is common to have number four across the street from number 294."

"My goodness! What a lot of walking you would have to do without getting directions first," Mother exclaimed, as she tasted another bite of brotvorst.

"Yes," he continued. "That is why I determined to ask the lifeguard. As I approached him, I heard a voice say, 'Go to Oppelner Strasse.' No one was around me and I knew it was the voice of the Spirit."

"I thought the Spirit warms your heart and speaks to you in that way," I said, trying not to sound too bewildered.

"It does sometimes, Karola, but there are times when the Spirit speaks with a voice as clear as yours and mine," Father explained patiently.

"Then what happened?" Ursula asked. She seemed eager for Father to continue his story, so that we could continue our meal.

Father looked around to be sure he had regained our full

attention. "I asked the lifeguard and found the addresses. This apartment is the one that I chose. But I'm going to save the other two and see why the Lord wanted us here."

"I like this apartment," said Esther.

"Actually, there was one I liked better, in our same branch and a little nicer I thought. But for some reason the Lord sent us here," said Father.

"I wonder why?" I mused.

"Only time will tell," Mother told me. "We'll just have to wait and see."

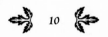

I have always enjoyed riding the subway, or U-Bahn as we called it, and as a child I really loved it! This particular trip was very special indeed. We were all together, except for Arno and his wife, Ruth, who had been married a short time before and lived in Leipzig. Another reason this trip was special was that we were going to hear Apostle Joseph Fielding Smith and his wife, Jessie Evans Smith, speak at a district conference.

It was the summer of 1939. I was nine years old. As we rode the U-Bahn, I listened to the constant chatter of my brothers and sisters. I felt the maturity of my years and added comments of my own. Now I chuckle to think about how I must have annoyed them with my remarks.

When we arrived at the conference, a large congregation had assembled. Father guided us to a row of chairs that still had enough vacant seats for our family. A tall man in front of me obstructed my view, and I immediately wished I had sat next to Mother.

"Do we have to sit in these same chairs through the whole conference?" I loudly asked Mother, two people away.

"Hush, Karola!" she sternly replied. I didn't understand why

I had to be quiet when everyone else in the whole building was talking.

"I can't whisper; you won't hear," I complained.

Mother had just opened her mouth to speak when a sudden stillness fell over the room. I looked around, wondering what had caused the silence, and saw Apostle Joseph Fielding Smith walking down the aisle.

I, too, was stunned into silence. He was a man of small stature, yet a great, majestic air was about him. My young heart knew with all the faith it contained that this man was indeed an apostle of the Lord Jesus Christ.

The stillness in the room remained all through Apostle Smith's sermon. I was impressed. I couldn't comprehend how such a large congregation could be so still and, though I couldn't understand all he said, I knew his words were true.

After the meeting was over and we were slowly moving toward the exit, I tried to watch every move Apostle Smith made. I climbed on a chair to see him over the heads and shoulders of other people, and not even Mother's frown could pull me away.

Riding the U-Bahn on the way home, Father and Mother gathered us around them. "We need to talk about what Apostle Smith said," Father explained. I was glad, since I hadn't understood it all.

"Joseph Fielding Smith has come from the prophet to warn all Europe of a coming war and to prepare us for a time when we will be cut off from the headquarters of the Church," Father solemnly informed us.

I watched the steadiness of Father's hands and his firm chin as he talked, faintly realizing how the burden of leadership would now weigh on his shoulders. Since our move to Berlin, he had been called as the branch president of the Neukoelln

Branch, and now he would be the sole shepherd of our little flock.

Mother turned to us, tears swimming in her eyes. "Oh, that I had wings and could fly to Zion," she sobbed. "Our American brothers will leave and we will have to stay!"

No one said a word. A solemn sadness overcame me. The only other time in my life that I had felt that way was on the train to Berlin when we left Horst standing alone at the station. I had wanted so badly to take him with us then. Now I longed to relieve Mother's anxiety and to tell her everything would be okay. But how could I? I couldn't supply the means to take our family to Zion. Her dearest wish was in vain, and I felt helpless.

The remainder of the trip was spent in painful silence. Mother, Father, and my older brothers and sisters held sober expressions and I felt their thoughts were solemn as well. However, I journeyed in silence to try to imagine what war was and how it could possibly affect my secure, happy life.

The last Sunday in August, as we came out of sacrament meeting, we were met by an unusual sight. Marching down the middle of the street was a group of German soldiers, not in any parade uniform, but in combat clothes, singing as they went.

People on both sides of the street went berserk. They waved, threw kisses, laughed, and sang with the soldiers. A current of excitement filled the air, making my own heart pound faster. It was as if the day had suddenly become a holiday and everyone had dropped whatever they were doing and started celebrating. Everywhere I looked, happy faces beamed—until I looked at Mother.

She gathered Esther and me close to her, as if trying to protect us from the scene. "Here they are going to war, joyful and laughing. When they come home there will be nothing but misery," she said, a sob choking her words.

A few days later we received a letter from Leipzig where Arno was living.

"Hurry, open it, Mother," cried Edith impatiently.

"What does he have to say?" asked Esther as she sat beside Mother at the table.

Mother's hands were still for a moment. She gravely looked at each of us before opening the letter. "Remember, there is a war."

In her wisdom, Mother prepared us for the worst. Perhaps she had a premonition of the contents of the letter. She unfolded the letter and read silently. Watching her reaction, I also knew. When Mother opened her mouth, I quickly covered my ears. I didn't want to hear, but the sound of Mother's voice still carried through my hands.

"He's been drafted," she said, her chin quivering slightly. "May the Lord be with us."

The news from Arno hung over us like black storm clouds. Days later, as I dressed for school, I recalled how happy life was when we lived in Leipzig. I wished I could find the clock that ticks away time and hold it back. Even if it meant that I would never grow up, the happy times would never change.

Just as Esther and I were leaving for school, Father walked in with the morning mail.

"A letter for Horst," he said, handing it to him. Horst was eating breakfast and didn't even look up.

Esther and I waited at the door to see what the letter contained.

Finally he opened the letter. Horst read quietly as we all watched him. Finally, he looked up and said with half a smile, "It looks as though the German army can't get along without me either."

Sorrow pulsed through my veins. Life would never be the same without Horst around to tease me.

"When do you have to go?" Mother anxiously asked.

"In the morning," he replied.

"Don't they give you time to pack?" I ignorantly asked.

Horst threw back his head and laughed. "No, Karola. I have to go in my pajamas."

Seeing my mistake and his eagerness to tease, I grabbed Esther's hand, heading for the hallway outside our apartment. As we closed the door, I heard Father say, "We'll help you get ready."

What a miserable, bleak day that was. Although the sun smiled down on me, unaware of the troubled world it lighted, I stubbornly refused to smile back. All day in school knots of pain twisted around in my stomach. I couldn't think, eat, or play. Horst would be leaving in the morning.

That night in my bed, I wished morning would never come. My bedroom was shadowy and terrifying. Though my eyes were open, darkness clouded my vision and I felt myself slipping away. I wanted to scream. All too quickly the night behind our bedroom curtains faded and the sun's rays peered in.

Horst burst into our bedroom. The door flew open so fast it banged into the wall, and Horst dropped his suitcase on the floor.

I stared at it soberly. It was a little bag, filled only with the necessities of a soldier, void of any comforts of home.

Horst broke into my solemn thoughts. "Why so gloomy?" he asked me. "Won't you be glad to finally have me out of the way?"

I shook my head vigorously.

Horst came to the side of my bed and asked, "Why not? Because I won't be here to put the bells under Father's bed so he makes nice music when it's time for sleeping?"

I laughed, remembering how angry Father got when Horst tied bells to his bedsprings.

"Remember the time I decided to put the ironing board under his sheets? 'AAAuuu!!!' Father screamed."

"And he jumped up and came straight for you, Horst," Edith reminded him, throwing her feather bed off. "He didn't even ask who did it—he knew."

"Yes," Horst laughed, shaking his head. "I suppose there will never be anyone else brave enough to make a fool out of Father."

I quickly looked at my parent's bedroom next door. If Father heard Horst talking disrespectfully, one final act of parental discipline would occur, even if Horst was twenty and going to war.

"Remember when I taught the missionaries some new German words?" Horst asked.

I shook my head as I threw my feather bed off and bounded happily on top of it.

"Oh, you know I taught them to say . . ."

"Shhh!" I whispered, putting my hand over his mouth. "Father will hear you."

"Oh, he can't spank me now. I'm a soldier." Horst gave a smart salute.

I giggled in spite of myself. "He'll probably still have to spank you when you're an old man."

"Very clever, Karola. But, you forget, when I'm an old man, Father will be even older. Can you imagine him trying to make me bend over to paddle my hollow trousers?"

The vision was hilarious, and I laughed until tears rolled down my cheeks. Horst continued his description, adding long gray beards and misplaced glasses until I could no longer breathe.

Mother entered our bedroom. "Horst, that's enough. You're killing her with your jokes," she told him. Turning to us she said, "Girls, get dressed quickly. Horst was up early and has already eaten. He doesn't have much time left."

My laughter stopped instantly. "I don't think I'll be able to have any breakfast; it would probably taste like sand."

Horst noted my gloominess and grabbed the feather bed I lay on, knocking me to the floor. He threw the feather bed over his shoulder. "Excuse me, Kaiserlein," he said. "I don't think the army will have feather beds like this. You'll have to loan me yours!"

My sisters giggled and I felt the smile return to my face. "Fine then," I said, pretending to pout and fold my arms across my chest.

"Horst, leave so the girls can dress," Mother ordered, pulling my feather bed away and pushing him out the door.

When the door closed she told us, "Horst tolerates happy tears much better than sad tears."

I quickly grabbed a light-blue blouse from my drawer and threw it over my head. As I struggled with the arms, I asked Mother, "Where will we go to tell Horst good-bye?"

She helped me pull the blouse down and said, "He will leave from here. He has to report to the draft board soon, but he won't take us with him. Some other young men from our apartment house will meet him by the front door and they'll go together."

"What about us?" I whined. "Can't we go?"

"Karola, most people say good-bye from home," Edith said. "Once the men are at the draft station, they're officially in the army."

We finished dressing and opened the door. Down the hallway Horst stood next to his small suitcase, waiting to say good-bye. The knots in my stomach were unbearable, and before I could think of being brave I was suddenly crying.

"Oh, Karola," Horst said tenderly. In a flash his arms were around me and my tears wet the front of his overcoat.

He gently smoothed my hair, still holding me while he kissed Father, Mother, and my sisters good-bye.

"God will be with you," Father told him while he firmly held Horst's hand. "Remember to call on the Lord; be faithful."

"Yes, Father," Horst reverently whispered. I thought his voice sounded hoarse, as if he might allow this tender farewell to evoke an emotion he rarely displayed. I looked up at him to see if he was crying as I was.

Horst bent down and wiped my tears with his handkerchief. "Don't cry for me, Karola. I'm going to come back and bother you more. You'll never be truly happy without me here to tease you. God knows that, and he'll let me return to torment you."

I opened my mouth to answer, but he swiftly slipped through the front door.

I cried even harder. I wanted to tell him that he was a pest, but I loved him dearly. I wanted to match wits with him and watch his pleasure when I came up with a good reply. I wanted to remember the times he had been mean or naughty, and laugh till my face turned blue. But it was too late. The laughter had stopped and the door clicked shut with him behind it.

CHAPTER 2

The monster screamed in pain, lashing out at Horst and trying to take away his sword. Horst stabbed the monster's side, and its piercing scream hurt my ears once more. I tried to inch myself further into the rock's crevice. Horst had told me not to move, but I had to escape that hideous scream. Just as it began to subside, Horst struck the beast again, and the scream erupted anew.

From far away I heard Mother's voice. "Quick girls!" she cried.

Horst lashed out at the monster; it screamed, but Mother's voice was strangely louder. "It's an air raid. We have to go down to the basement."

"What do we take?" Edith sleepily asked, throwing off her covers.

I sat up in bed and tried to open my eyes.

"Put on a robe, and you better take an extra blanket, I guess," Mother instructed.

Esther hit my face with her robe, struggling to put it on.

"Ouch! That's my face!" I cried.

"Never mind that, Karola. Hurry and get your robe on," Edith ordered as she bumped into Ursula.

I rushed around the bedroom in the dark trying to hurry and taking twice as long.

"Come, let's go!" Father cried. His voice still held authority, but there was an anxious strain in the pitch. At last we emerged from the bedroom.

"Where do we go?" I asked.

"Follow me to the basement," Mother replied. Edith, Ursula, Esther, and I began to follow.

Just outside the apartment door, I turned and waited for Father to lock the front door. As I watched him, I became aware of how strange my surroundings were. Eerie shadows slithered on the walls; the sirens that awoke me still screamed on the same note as the terrible monster. Cool air, like icy fingers, crept along my skin, and a shiver rushed down my spine. My stomach felt like it had been turned inside out. My head spun 'round and 'round, as if it were sliding down the banister of a spiral staircase.

"I feel funny . . ." I mumbled as darkness engulfed me.

When I awoke, it was morning. I was back in my own bed. Mother must have let me sleep in because the sun was well on its way across the sky. I barely remembered our middle-of-the-night outing. It almost seemed like a miserable nightmare.

I heard voices coming from the kitchen. It sounded as if the family was having lunch, although I was certain I hadn't slept in that late. I crawled out of bed, my stomach growling fiercely, telling me I couldn't afford to miss breakfast, or lunch for that matter.

"Karola is not getting enough to eat, and now having her sleep interrupted . . ." there was a pause, and I heard a heavy sigh. "She'll never be healthy. She's only nine years old and still in her growing years," Mother was saying as I entered the kitchen.

"Good morning everyone," I said, trying to sound cheerful.

My family was gathered around the kitchen table, sitting in their usual places. The only dish on the table was mine. It was empty. Mother must have been keeping my breakfast mush warm on the stove.

"We're not going to the basement anymore," Esther informed me.

I stared at them in surprise. What were they thinking? Weeks ago I'd heard announcements over the radio urging us to hurry to shelter the instant sirens started.

"Why not?" I asked Mother, the lumpy mush sticking to my throat.

"You're too little to have your sleep interrupted," said Ursula.

Father cleared his throat to announce that he would speak. "Last night you fainted," he began. "When I finished locking the door, I turned around and just caught you."

I thought back, trying to remember the moments before darkness closed over me. Yes, Father must have saved me from a bad fall when I fainted.

"Your mother has decided that we should all stay up here and let the bombs fall. They didn't even come to our part of the city last night," Father explained.

I looked at Mother and opened my mouth to speak.

"Get dressed, Karola," Mother quickly said as she cut a slice of hard brown bread. "Then you can eat some bread if you're still hungry."

"Mother, what will we do when the bombs fall?" I asked fearfully, not wanting to let the subject rest just yet. "If we're up here, we could be killed!"

Mother stopped slicing and looked at me intently. "My mind is made up," she said sternly. "It's too hard for you to go down there in the middle of the night. We'll just stay in our beds."

I stumbled from the kitchen in a daze, hardly knowing what to think. I didn't want to be the cause of my family's staying upstairs where it was too dangerous. But I knew better than to argue with Mother. When she acted like that, the decision was final. No one said another word about it, especially not me.

That night the monster started screaming again. This time I was wide awake, waiting and ready. I heard doors slamming and the hasty shuffling of feet as other people hurried to safety. I closed my eyes and prayed that Mother knew what she was doing by keeping us upstairs.

When the last door was slammed shut and all the footsteps faded away in the night, a strange stillness settled over the city. I strained every muscle to hear something. The quiet was dreadful. I wondered if you could hear a bomb if it lands directly on top of you. Can you hear it coming, or is everything over before you know it's even started?

From way up in the sky I heard a shrill whistle. It grew louder and louder, coming fast and steady. In a flash the silence exploded around me. The room lit up for an instant, and I saw that my sisters were also awake, wide-eyed and terrified.

I let my breath out all at once. It felt good to breathe again. I didn't realize how hard I was straining to hear that first explosion.

Another followed soon and then another, and another, and another. They became deafening and powerful. There was no time between them; as one ended, another began. It was as if they were trying to outdo each another, until I couldn't even hear the warning whistle anymore.

Our beds began to sway; the whole apartment building shook. I sat up and looked anxiously through the doorway to my parents' bedroom. Surely Mother would come any minute and tell us to go downstairs.

"Go to sleep girls," she said, almost as if she had heard my thoughts. "Everything will be all right."

How could she know everything would be all right? Was there a way to tell? Perhaps she had prayed and received an answer. That was possible. Mother prayed differently than other people. When she prayed she talked to the Lord as if he were right beside her.

Somehow, hearing her say everything would be all right made me believe it was true. I laid back down on my pillow and closed my eyes. Bombs fell, beds swayed, my ears were ringing with the noise, but my heart was calm. I wondered how I would ever sleep through it all, and then the morning sun was shining through the windows.

It was Saturday. I jumped out of bed and bounded into the kitchen. Mother would be going shopping today and I wanted to be the first to ask if I could come along. That would increase my chances of going.

Actually, what she did was shop with ration cards. She would stand in line hoping the store wouldn't run out of what we needed before it was her turn. If she was fortunate enough to receive what the ration card said she should, she would pay with the cards and a little money. Still, it was fun for me. It was a chance to get out of the apartment and, possibly, most of the Saturday chores.

"Can I go shopping with you today, Mutter?" I blurted when I entered the kitchen.

"My goodness, Karola!" Mother exclaimed. "Not so much as a 'good morning' and still in your pajamas."

"I'll get dressed," I obediently told her. "I just wanted to know if I could go . . ."

"It might be quite a while," she warned, brushing loose strands of hair out of her face.

"I don't care," I answered jumping up and down, unable to control my excitement.

"Karola," Father muttered, when he entered the kitchen. Although I knew he was disappointed in my behavior, I also knew he wouldn't get angry. Horst named me well when he called me *Kaiserlein*, meaning "little empress."

"Can I go, Mutter? Can I? Can I?" I begged.

Mother sighed with exasperation. "All right."

I dressed swiftly and ate my dry, brown bread as if it were wheat toast with honey.

"Karola, you have to clear the dishes into the tub under the table and sweep the floor while Mother gets ready to go," Edith ordered. We stored the dirty dishes under the table until the end of the day. This way, we had to wash them only once since it took a long time to heat water in the large pans on the stove.

"Why?" I whined.

"Because you don't have to stay and help with Saturday chores," she said.

I couldn't argue with that logic and I didn't want to. Dishes clattered, cups rattled, water sloshed, dirt flew, and in a few moments I was out the door with Mother.

Skipping merrily along beside her, I barely noticed the grave look the other Saturday shoppers had; there wasn't a single smiling face among them. It was as if each had a dark cloud hovering over his or her head.

As we neared the grocery store, I noticed an apartment house that had been hit by bombs. What had been a grand building was now a scorched skeleton, bare and stagnant. I stopped skipping and stared at the lonely, forbidding place.

"Where are the people that used to live there?" I asked Mother.

"Gone," was the only information she gave. We were at the

store, and the line already went as far back as the entrance doors.

I didn't like waiting outside with that skeleton looming over me.

"Well, the war won't last long," said a voice behind me. I turned to see a round little woman wearing a loose-fitting dress with a faded blue sweater.

"Hitler has the Allies by the throat," she said, looking around for approval from others in the line. Some nodded their agreement, some looked down or turned away.

I looked at Mother to see her reaction. She shook her head at me ever so slightly and pretended not to hear the conversation behind us.

Encouraged by the amount of support she seemed to be getting, the woman continued discussing the war and what looked like a sure German victory. People in line began to agree; it was strange to me that no one disagreed with her.

I tried not to stare at her, but I felt I had to watch every move she made, the way one would watch a vicious barking dog, wondering if it will attack.

The line to the grocery counter seemed to be moving backward. "How long have we been waiting?" I asked Mother.

"I warned that it would take a while," she said.

"I know," I answered unhappily. "How much longer do we have to wait?"

"We haven't been waiting very long, Karola. Only fifteen minutes."

Fifteen minutes! Was that all? I wondered if I could stand hearing the woman much longer. Her face became red and she slapped her fist in the palm of her hand to emphasize her words. She must have been able to tell that some people in line didn't agree with all she said. Perspiration spotted her forehead and she desperately tried to convince them that her views were right. As she wiped her forehead with a crinkled gray handker-chief, the line moved forward again and we were inside.

A few minutes later, Mother was showing the clerk her ration cards. He was already out of a few of the items, but we managed to fill our shopping nets with a meager supply of gro-ceries. Mother returned the rest of the ration cards to her purse and let me carry one of the grocery nets from the store.

As soon as we were out of range of the people waiting, I decided it was a safe time to ask Mother why she hadn't told the people what she thought. I knew Mother could have helped the lady with the blue sweater understand what was wrong with her views, leaving no room for questions.

"It's too dangerous," she replied. "If we're winning the war, Hitler is winning, and we don't support him. If we're losing the war, Hitler is losing and his nonsupporters will pay the price. Either way, we must be quiet and just do the Lord's work."

I didn't say anything the rest of the way home. It hadn't occurred to me that we were living in such a dangerous place that one couldn't even say how he really felt. I thought of my father and the bravery he showed when he told the Nazi party he had chosen to serve Jesus Christ. Our whole family had to pay the price while Father went without work. But Father and Mother weren't afraid to show their devotion to the Lord.

❖ ❖

A clutter of pans in the kitchen woke me suddenly. I sat up in bed staring at my surroundings. Something was different. I remembered going to bed excited, but my dreams had erased my memory of something wonderful that was to happen today.

"Be sure and fix plenty," Father was telling Mother.

Horst! I jumped out of bed. My memory had returned and

came crashing down on me like a giant ocean wave. Horst would be coming home today!

A week earlier he had written to tell us he would be coming home on furlough to get married. Mother had kept most of this a secret from me until just a few days ago. I guess she knew that in my great excitement I wouldn't allow her a moment's rest and that she wouldn't be able to make the necessary preparations.

The night before I was finally told when he would be here. I couldn't sleep for hours and then, strangely, I had forgotten all together. Until now—now I remembered he would be here in time for breakfast.

I dressed quickly and was combing my hair when the front door opened.

Everyone scrambled towards him at once, but I out ran them all. We became a giant ball of people, pulling and hugging Horst. Somehow we managed to move away from the entrance and everyone let go of him to get a good look. Everyone, that is, but me.

It was April 1941. Horst had been gone almost two years. I had dreamed of this moment for so long I just couldn't let it pass by. I could tell that the army hadn't fed him very well—my arms reached further around him than before. His uniform smelled of smoke mixed with coffee, and I knew he had been on the train. He was still breathing more heavily than normal, so he must have run all the way home.

"Karola, get back so we can all see Horst," said Ursula.

I wanted to see him, too, so finally I stepped back.

He was crying. Not loud and obviously, the way some people do, but his face muscles strained as he tried to hold a steady look, and his eyes were moist and red.

I was just about to rush back into his arms when I remembered how Mother had once said that Horst liked happy tears better than sad ones. So I blurted, "My goodness, have you been carrying onions?"

"Karola!" Mother scolded, but it did the trick. Horst burst out laughing and pulled me to his side. "You'll never know how much I really missed you, my little Kaiserlein."

"Quick then," Mother cried, clapping her hands to hurry us along. "You'll just have time for breakfast before going to the courthouse."

We all gathered around the table, blessed the food, and started eating. After seeing the way Horst was shoveling his breakfast down, I was glad that Father had told Mother to fix plenty. He must have remembered how good Mother's cooking was after eating army rations.

"How are you getting married?" I asked Horst when I had swallowed my last mouthful.

Horst's eyes twinkled, but his mouth was full, hindering him from laughing at my question the way he would have liked.

Mother supplied the answer for him. "He'll take Irene to the courthouse before a judge." She answered me quickly as if talking fast would help me understand. "Afterwards, he'll bring her to the Church's meeting place. There they will change into white clothes and be married for time by your father. Then we'll have a nice luncheon."

"Is that what happened when you and Father were married?" I wondered.

"Goodness no, Karola," Mother replied, pushing away from the table and clearing her spot. "Since Father was Lutheran and I was Catholic, we didn't get married by anyone holding the priesthood. But, if the good Lord grants that we go to America, we can be sealed together in the temple."

"So Horst and Irene won't be sealed, either," I said.

"Sealings for time and eternity can be done only in the temple by a man who holds the priesthood," Father told me.

I nodded my head as I began to comprehend the information given me.

Horst rose from his place and wiped his mouth on the back of his hand since we hadn't supplied a cloth napkin. Laundry soap was rationed too, and we were cutting back everywhere we could.

I also jumped up from my spot and hurried to put the dishes in the tub under the table. Cups rattled, bowls clanked, the broom made a swishing sound as Edith swept, and everyone did his or her part to help the busy day start off well.

When I finished the dishes, Horst was in the entry just getting ready to leave. I hurried to him and tugged on his arm. He bent over to look right into my face, and I winked and whispered, "Good luck."

His laugh told me again that he had missed me. He patted my head and was out the door.

We dressed in our best clothes and hastened to the Church's rented meeting place, which was a concert hall in the evenings. We carefully set up a nice luncheon upstairs for family and friends. When we finished and Mother had inspected our efforts, we were allowed to wait quietly for Horst and his new bride, Irene, downstairs in the area we used as the sacrament meeting room.

People began filing into the rented building. It seemed to me that everyone's face was aglow with excitement and cheer. I thought that they must have put aside their own misfortunes for the day to enjoy the happiness that Horst and Irene would share.

We didn't wait long. A shout went up from the congregation. The happy couple entered the large room and everyone surrounded them, shaking hands, patting backs, wiping eyes, and offering their congratulations.

When everyone quieted, Father stood in front of those

assembled and motioned for Horst and Irene to face him. Just as Mother said, there was a brief ceremony while Father married them the second time that day. At first I thought it strange that they should be married twice in one day, but when I looked at the expressions on Horst and Irene's faces, I thought of something I hadn't realized before. Father spoke words of wisdom and loving counsel to them that I was certain the official at the courthouse would never have said. His advice helped their wedding day become a celebration. Their marriage certificate would have special meaning and be more to them then just a piece of paper. Although they weren't being married forever, they were given counsel to lay the foundations of a temple marriage.

When Father finished, Horst tenderly kissed Irene and everyone clapped happily. At last Horst guided his bride upstairs for the luncheon. They settled at the head of a table while everyone scurried to find a seat. Father gave a short speech of official congratulations, and the luncheon began.

I caught a glimpse of Horst laughing with Irene. I tried to catch his eye and smile or wink at him, but he didn't look at me. In the bustle that followed, I suddenly realized that Horst wouldn't be my big brother the way he used to. He would have a family now, his own children to tease. Things would never be the same again.

Why does time keep ticking when the future only takes loved ones away? I didn't want him to go. And during the commotion of his marriage, I was forgotten, and the next thing I knew he and Irene had eaten and were gone.

"What's the matter?" asked Esther, taking my hand as she noticed my gloominess.

"Horst is gone, and I never got a chance to say good-bye," I mumbled, trying hard not to cry like a baby.

"But this isn't good-bye—we will see him again," Esther explained.

"It won't ever be the same," I sobbed.

"If life were always the same, it would get very dull, even with Horst around."

I looked at her with awe-filled eyes. Every once in a while Esther amazed me. There were times when she knew just what to say or do to soothe my troubled heart.

Now I realized she was right. Life had to move forward, and when it did, Horst would be there once more.

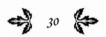

Sunday morning dawned with an early chill. My toes were numb under the covers and it hurt to step out of bed. As I sat rubbing some feeling back into them, I naughtily wished I didn't have to go to church on such a cold day.

The walk to church took forty-five minutes and on a day like this it seemed endless. Added to this was the fact that we didn't go to church just once on Sunday, but *twice*. That long, treacherous walk was repeated four times before the day was through.

As we began our first journey for the day, chilling wind blew through me and my breath froze on my scarf. I remembered how Horst used to spit just to hear it land on the sidewalk already frozen. The thought warmed me for an instant before the wind numbed my thoughts again.

After Sunday School, I was the first one home. I wasn't old enough to be embarrassed by running down the street. My poor sisters walked home dignified and very cold.

In the bedroom I had curled into a tiny ball on my bed, desperately trying to get warm, when I heard the front door shut with a strange bang. I jumped up and raced to the entry, nearly colliding with Father.

When he brushed by he mumbled, "Bitte," as though in another world. His behavior intrigued me and I watched his every move.

He went to his paints and took out a heavy piece of paper, then mixed up some dark brown paint and, in his slender grand script, began writing.

I carefully crept closer. Mother and my sisters walked in. I quickly put my finger to my lips, signaling them to silence. He was so engrossed in his work, I didn't dare disturb him. It wasn't until the graceful letters began to dry and his brush remained motionless, poised above the paper, that I dared to ask, "What is it for, Father?"

A slow smile curved the corners of his mouth when he replied, "The meeting place."

"Why?"

Father rinsed his brush clean and laid it back in his paint paraphernalia before he answered, "So that people will remember whose house it is that we worship in."

He left me in the kitchen to ponder his response a moment. I looked at the drying words on the paper. They said, " . . . and establish a house, even a house of prayer, a house of fasting, a house of faith, a house of learning, a house of glory, a house of order, a house of God— D&C 88:119." After studying the scripture a moment, I went after Father. He was sitting in the front room, waiting for me.

Before I could speak, he said, "Come, sit down, Karola. I'll tell you what happened."

I sat close beside him while Esther, Ursula, and Edith filed in. I guessed they had heard Father and didn't want to miss out on the story.

"When I entered the meeting place today, I noticed one

31

sweet elderly sister busily hammering a nail in the wall," Father began.

"Which sister?" I wanted to know.

"Never mind, that's unimportant." Father erased my question with a wave of his hand. "When she stood back to admire her work, I found it difficult to control my surprise. She had just finished hanging a picture of Adolph Hitler."

"Meine gute!" exclaimed Mother from the kitchen. I hadn't noticed before that she was listening.

"Oh, Father!" Edith gasped. "What on earth did you do?"

Father smiled and said, "Well, you understand that all the other churches display pictures of Hitler—I suppose she thought we should, too."

"If they all do it, that doesn't make it right," Mother said, more for my benefit than anything else I think.

Father continued, "I very kindly removed the picture and handed it back to her. 'Sister,' I explained, 'this man has no place in our Heavenly Father's house.'"

"Oh, you handled that well," Mother said with a sigh.

"I'm not finished," Father raised his eyebrows in annoyance. "I told her that this man has no place in our Heavenly Father's house, not unless he repents and is baptized."

"What did she do?" I asked excitedly.

"She graciously took the picture away."

"What if she says something about it?" Ursula wondered. "There could be dreadful consequences."

"If she reports the incident, I will not deny it. Although I could be taken to a concentration camp, I will accept the consequences," Father firmly told her.

My stomach felt like I had swallowed a live rabbit. I left the room, feeling my way because I couldn't see clearly. I wasn't sure I could handle anymore consequences due to Father's bravery. In my bedroom I lay on my bed and tried to clear my mind.

Someone on the floor above me must have had a lot on his mind, too. That someone constantly paced back and forth, making it difficult for me to rest. My mind was such a muddled mess that I stayed in my room until it was time to get ready for the long walk back to church for sacrament meeting.

During sacrament meeting I noticed that Father had hung his new artwork on the nail the good sister had provided. Father reminded everyone to treat the room as the house of the Lord, since it was dedicated to His service, even though it was just a rented building and not a church.

On a Sunday in June 1941, Father left early as usual but returned a while later. When he entered the apartment, his face was deathly white.

"What's the matter?" Mother anxiously asked.

Hearing her voice, I jumped out of bed and ran to the kitchen with my sisters.

We stood there rubbing our bare feet together to keep them warm, waiting for Father to tell us.

"This morning the Germans marched into Russia. Now we know why the boys have been transferred to the East." He sat weakly down at the kitchen table.

My sisters and I clung to each other, not knowing what to say. It seemed so unreal. But from the expression on my parents' faces, I knew it was terribly real. My brothers had gone off to war, to fight or be killed.

"That fool Sergeant Hitler is fighting the whole world!" exclaimed Father. "We have won a few battles and the others will win the war. No country can survive battling on all her fronts."

CHAPTER 3

I was still sick inside, but not the kind that would allow me to stay home from church. I sat unusually quiet on my hard fold-up chair and stared at the poster Father had made two years earlier. The words could offer comfort, but I refused to let them.

Tears fell around me, but I was angry and refused that first step to heal. I would build a granite wall around my hurt, and nothing could reach my sorrow and help it to escape. I wanted it that way; it was only fair that I should never smile until my brothers returned safely home.

I noticed a man sitting towards the front. He turned in his chair and watched people find their seats. His eyes were clouded with inward pain. He must have felt me watch him. He looked at me, our eyes locked in a stare, and he saw my misery.

I turned away from his scrutinizing gaze with a start, angry that someone had broken through my fortress and shared my suffering. Although I felt his eyes on me, I ignored him. Why should a grown man stare at a little girl? Why didn't he look away?

I couldn't listen. Without wanting to I began wondering why the man was feeling as miserable as I. His clothes were threadbare, but so were mine. Surely his life was in turmoil, but mine was, too. He looked hungry, as was I. When he turned to the front, I studied him intently. He sat alone, two rows in front of me.

My eyes were wet; I bit my lip hard to keep from crying out loud. He was alone. I at least had part of my family with me. Even if he was an adult, I didn't think he should be alone.

After the meeting I pushed my way through the people cluttering the aisles to reach his chair. His head was still bowed as if he hadn't heard the amens to the closing prayer. Gently I tugged on his sleeve.

"Bitte, bitte," I begged.

He looked at me with pain-filled eyes. "What is it?" he asked in pitifully poor German. A strange pain closed over my chest, making it difficult for me to speak. I wanted to somehow make his sorrow easier to bear.

"Come to our house for dinner," I said. "My mutter welcomes everyone who has no place to go."

"I don't know your mutter," he tried to explain.

"That doesn't matter," I blurted, vigorously shaking my head. "You are welcome; you must come, bitte."

In his eyes I saw the tiniest twinkle as he tried to smile. "Danke."

Mother seemed surprised to see me boldly leading the young foreign worker towards her. I had never asked anyone to dinner before—Mother usually did.

"This man is hungry, Mother," I told her.

She smiled at him. "There is room at our table." Looking down at me, her eyes sparkled. "Karola will show you the way," she added.

At our dinner table he ate slowly and very politely, yet I knew inside he was starving, aching to shove each mouthful in and swallow it whole. It felt so good to see him eat.

"My goodness!" I exclaimed aloud. Everyone stared at me

and I smiled inwardly. "This is a wonderful dinner," I said, but I didn't explain my secret. What had made it so grand was that we had someone to share it with. I realized that my anger was gone. In its place was something much nicer and perhaps even more powerful.

Several Sundays later we had another foreign worker visit our home. While Mucky (Mooh-key) visited with Edith, I stole away to the kitchen where Mother was putting the finishing touches on our Sunday meal. Leaning up beside her, I reached for the bread knife she held in her hand.

"I'll slice the bread," I offered.

"I'm nearly finished," she replied. Then seeing my disappointment, she quickly added, "You can get a plate to put the slices on."

As I reached for the plate I allowed the question I had been turning over in my mind to slip past my lips. "Why are the foreign workers in Berlin?"

"They're here to free the German men for fighting," she replied, brushing a stray brown strand of hair from my face.

The smell of the evening's broth bubbling on the stove made my stomach growl audibly. Mother looked sideways at me. I pretended not to notice and asked, "What do they do?"

"Everything from replacing German men in the factories to keeping things in working order. Anything that needs to be done."

"Do they want to be here?"

"Don't you think you could answer that?"

I smiled at her. "Yes, they look so sad and forlorn, I know they'd rather be home. Do they have to be here? Does Hitler hold them against their will? Don't they get paid?"

Mother sighed heavily at my many questions. "Karola, Karola, they have to work. They are like prisoners."

"Poor Joe and Martin," I said, shaking my head in pity. Joe

Rhynsburger and Martin Sarris were two workers from Holland whom we had come to know and love. "I'm sure they deserve better," I observed.

"My dear, we all do," Mother reminded me as she finished slicing the last of the bread. "Go ahead and put the bread on the table, Karola," she instructed. "I'll just be a few minutes to finish in here. You can wait with the others if you'd like."

I unhappily went to the couch and picked up a book I had read three times before. As I read, I thought about Joe, Martin, and Mucky. Mucky's real name was Zdeneck Krecheck, and he was a Czechoslovakian. Because his name was so hard to pronounce we called him Mucky. He came to our home because he liked Edith. She denied that was his reason, but I knew better. His face spoke loudly of his love every time he looked in her direction.

Mucky was Catholic. Edith invited him to go to church and soon he was baptized. He usually came home with us after sacrament meeting, and today was no exception.

"Where's your father today?" Mucky asked. He was asking Edith, but I chimed in, "Didn't you pay attention in sacrament meeting? He's out of town with his company."

"Oh," he replied, turning red around the collar.

"You should listen in church, not watch Edith," I teased.

"Karola," Mother gently reprimanded. "Time to set the table. Come get the plates please."

I slammed my book shut and dragged myself to the kitchen. With Horst gone it had become so difficult to find someone to match wits with. Mucky didn't seem to mind my teasing, so I couldn't see why I had to be ushered out of the way.

I grabbed the stack of bowls and hurried to the table, Esther following close behind with utensils. We made a grand show for Mucky as we set the table. Esther hummed, I talked, Mother muttered, "Girls, girls," Ursula giggled, and Edith sighed with exasperation.

Dinner didn't turn out any differently. It seemed we all wanted to make an impression for our company.

After dinner and dishes, we settled around the piano while Mother sat in her favorite chair and set her comfortable, worn-out house shoes by the stove to warm.

Sunday evenings were so grand. Esther played the piano that had seen many days since its last thorough tuning, and we all tried to harmonize singing hymns. When Father and Horst were with us, we sounded almost as grand as a great choir. The foreign workers may not have been able to speak good German, but if they spent time at our house they could always sing the hymns.

At these times especially, I missed Horst. With him at my side I could sing no matter what color the clouds above were. He and I would be able to tease Mucky and Edith until it would be a wonder if Mucky ever came to our home again.

"It's nearly ten o'clock," Mother gently hinted at evening's end.

"Yes, I guess it is time for me to go," said Mucky, smiling at Edith.

Edith opened her mouth to answer, but was cut off by the sound of the air raid siren.

"Where is your basement?" Mucky asked. "Let's go!" He snatched his hat from the hook in the entry.

"Calm down, Mucky," said Edith waving his anxiety away with a flick of her hand. "There's no rush."

"We haven't been to a shelter in years. Karola gets sick if we do," Ursula explained.

"Besides, who is afraid of a little bombing!" I scoffed with a laugh at Mucky's bewilderment.

"What's the matter?" I continued. "Is a big, strong man like

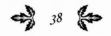

you scared? Why, I'm just a girl and I'm not shaking." I held my hands steady in front of me to prove it.

"I don't . . . I mean, why do you . . ." he stammered.

Mother suddenly jumped up. "Hurry, hurry, hurry, girls, we have to run!" She gathered us like a hen gathers her chicks when there is danger and hurried all of us down the four stories, out the back way, across the open courtyard and down the twelve metal steps to the basement.

As she took her foot off the last step, there was a terrifying crash. Everything went black and something fluffy started falling from the ceiling.

"A light? Doesn't anyone have a candle?" asked a frightened voice.

My heart was pounding so loudly my ears pulsed. Someone found a candle, and a timid light fell on us. I could see that everyone was literally white. Our hair, faces, and clothes were covered in a thin film of paint from the ceiling. The white was still gently fluttering down on top of us. A small girl was crying and holding to her mother's skirt, but no one seemed to be hurt.

I tried to talk but didn't trust my voice. For a few moments no one said a word, and I guessed they felt as shaken up as I did.

"Let's see what happened!" I said, suddenly snapping to reality. I bounded up the steps before Mother could stop me. My sisters followed on my heels.

I felt like I had swallowed cold black mud when I looked at the scene before me. The apartment house across the street had received a total hit. Already the building was a terrible inferno, a death trap to those who hadn't left their apartments. My mouth gaped open in horror as I saw mothers push their children through upper story windows before they themselves leaped from the fire in panic. People in the streets screamed at them, then tried to catch them, but . . .

A strong arm jerked me away from the door. "You better

check your apartment," Mucky firmly told me. He pushed me towards Mother before he ran across the street to help.

All the way up the stairs, the terrible scene outside replayed itself in my mind. Shouting still rang through the streets. Even when I covered my ears it was audible.

Mother was behind me in the stairwell. She pulled me to a stop and flung her arms around me. "If only I could have spared you that," she whispered. I felt her tears wet my hair and her hand shake as she softly stroked my hair.

I looked up at her, too shocked to cry. "Why couldn't the people catch them?"

Mother's lower lip trembled when she replied, "There wasn't time to prepare." I nodded that I understood. Nets and blankets couldn't be spread quickly enough before the vicious flames tortured their victims into preferring a frantic leap to excruciating burning.

Mother and I continued to our apartment in silence.

The stunning shock of what I had seen across the street gave way to tears when I saw our apartment. What a disaster! The windows were shattered and glass covered the floor. The outside wall had an enormous indentation, as if it were too weak to hold back some massive blast.

"How in the world did this happen?" I cried, spreading my hands in a helpless gesture.

Mother slowly shook her head. "The tremendous force of air pressure."

"Air did that?" I asked somewhat puzzled.

"Karola, a bomb landed just across the street," said Ursula. She scrutinized the shattered window where torn curtains flapped clumsily in a breeze that smelled of smoke and death.

"We obviously would have been killed had we remained," Edith softly whispered, as though speaking too loudly might change the events that had just occurred.

"Oh, Mother," Esther cried turning towards her. "You were inspired to guide us away from here."

"Yes," Mother said softly, "let us thank the Lord for his protection and blessing."

We brushed the glass away to clear a spot for our family prayer. I marveled at how in tune Mother was so that when the Spirit whispered, even in a room full of laughing girls, she had heard and obeyed.

From that time on, we went to the basement at the sound of the air raid sirens. It was 1943.

❈ ❈

One evening I tried again to mend a hole in my stocking. Among the gray, brown, and light blue thread that covered the hole, there was barely a trace of the original white color left.

Esther played the piano in a world that was far beyond Berlin. The mood of her music fit the homely atmosphere we shared. It was quiet, peaceful, and cozy. Edith and Ursula sat on the couch whispering together under the pretense of sharing a book. Mother was trying to read, at least the way her lips were forming words one might be led to believe she was. But her eyes never moved across the page. She seemed to be concentrating on a war going on in her mind. At times her face carried such an expression, I often thought that she was praying with her whole soul.

Father cleared his throat several times in succession, and we all knew he had something important to tell us. I dropped my sewing, Mother's face cleared, and Edith and Ursula closed their book. But Esther didn't hear. She continued to play.

Edith and Ursula nudged each other to keep from giggling out loud as Father again cleared his throat for our undivided attention.

"Esther," Mother softly called. "Esther, quiet there."

It didn't work—she was still in a trance. We had nicknamed her Ludwiga, for Ludwig van Beethoven, since the music seemed to cast a spell over her and only physical contact could arouse her from its grasp.

Before Father could get angry, I hurried to the piano. I reached out my hand to shake her but, changing my mind, I placed both hands under her arms and pinched her instead.

"Youch!" she squealed. Edith exploded with laughter, Mother grinned, Ursula giggled, and Father looked exasperated.

I crept back to the couch, and Esther followed, rubbing under her arms. When at last our merry family room had quieted to a sober chamber, Father began. "My company will be leaving for Thuringen."

The silence in the room was eerie. I didn't dare speak. Seeing the wide, worried eyes of my sisters, I was sure they felt as forsaken as I did. Father's short sentence seemed to drop a bomb of despair over us. With Father away, there would be no priesthood in our home. No more much-needed blessings. Indeed, I felt abandoned, bewildered, and alone.

"With the bombing as heavy as it has become, all companies are leaving Berlin for obvious safety reasons," Father solemnly explained.

"That means the school children will soon follow," observed Mother, folding her hands across the book in her lap.

My heart leaped to my throat like a cat springs to a table. It was my last year of school, and if the school children had to leave, that meant I would be the only one from our family going. I wanted to scream a protest, but strangely my mouth wouldn't move.

"How long will you be gone?" I heard Esther ask Father.

"As long as they say. I don't know. I should be able to come home for visits."

"How often?" she asked.

"Oh, perhaps once or twice a month."

I looked at Mother. She had aged greatly since the war began. Thick stripes of gray now colored her hair and worry lines accented her face. Would she still be strong with Father so far away? I wondered. I wanted to speak to her, to beg her not to send me away with the school children, but her face looked so weary and careworn, I couldn't bother her with my problems now. She had a more immense crisis to worry over.

"I'm going to bed," I announced when my mouth finally began working again. This talk was terribly upsetting to me. I suppose at thirteen it was too much to have brothers and now Father taken away.

"That's a good idea," Father acknowledged. "Let's kneel for prayer."

We numbly kneeled as Father's clear, strong voice expressed to our Heavenly Father the anxieties we shared. No sniffles or sobs escaped our lips; we were brave and sure until Father's voice broke and his prayer stopped short. A long silence followed like the calm before a storm. He tried to speak again, and I couldn't hold it in any longer. My cry collided with wails, sobs, and moans from my mother and sisters.

Still kneeling, we put our arms around each other as Father literally cried to the Lord for our welfare and protection.

The prayer finished, and our cries continued; but strangely, a warm feeling was slowly spreading from my heart to my whole being. It was as if a quiet hand had closed itself over mine, giving my whole body a peace I could not understand.

A few days later we were at the train station. I wondered if I could ever shed tears of joy at such a place. Trains take away loved ones, but do they ever bring them back? Filthy soot covered everything and seemed to blanket my being as well.

Loneliness was trying to crowd the peace that had engulfed

me. I tried not to let it win, but seeing Father quietly holding Mother next to him made it very difficult. Father was not like Horst. On such a serious occasion he didn't mind tears of despair. It was an easy job to show him how much he would be missed.

The train whistle blew, startling fresh tears from my eyes. Father kissed Edith first, then Ursula, Esther, and Mother. I knew he saved the last kiss good-bye for me because I was the youngest, but also I thought because I was his Kaiserlein—his little girl that he would rather spoil than spank.

"You will be all grown up when I return," Father solemnly told me. A sad look clouded his eyes.

"But you will come home for visits," I said, trying to sound reassuring. "It will not happen too fast."

He studied me for a long moment. "It already has."

The train waited for another minute while Father boarded. We strained to see his face through a soot-covered window, but it didn't appear. I wondered why, and then I realized how brave he truly was. He hadn't cried since that night during our farewell prayer. Now, at last, he had a moment alone. I felt sure he had found a solitary seat to support his fatigued body, and while others on the train cried their good-byes through the windows, he cried to himself when no one would notice. When they finished weeping and settled in their seats, he would again hold the look of a firm, undaunted man. Perhaps only the small trickle of a tear would give a hint that he had just repeated a prayer similar to the one he had held with his family a few nights ago.

How dearly I loved him! My strong, stalwart father, who outwardly showed us bravery but inwardly was frightened, too. Not many men of any religion would stand before representatives of the Nazi party and declare allegiance to Jesus Christ rather than Hitler. Yet that was what my father had done. Even though we had paid a dear price for it, none of us regretted how gallant a man our father was. As we made our way home, I held my head erect and proud. No one would have thought that I had just kissed my father good-bye at the train station. I wouldn't wear my troubles on my sleeve for all to see. My valiant father would be proud of his little Kaiserlein.

Several days later, as we gathered in the family room for our nightly ritual of reading, sewing, and listening to Esther at the piano, Edith read war news from a newspaper she had found at work. It was only one day old, and the information was still current. We listened quietly, hoping and praying that our dear Horst and Arno had made it through another day of chaos. At last she finished the headlines, and we began to settle again into our cozy atmosphere, as no unsettling news was read. Edith held her thumb between pages, ready to turn, when the announcement she read brought my head up sharply from my sewing. I stared at her, hoping I wasn't hearing correctly. She felt my stare and looked over her paper into my eyes. Her eyes filled with sympathy and she repeated the announcement for the benefit of everyone else in the room. Anxiety swirled around me like a whirlwind. The schools were going to close. All school children and teachers would be moved to Bavaria and other outlying areas. My most dreaded fear was being realized.

Mother watched my fear-stricken face and pressed her lips into a tight line.

"Don't worry, Karola," she said, soothing away my fears. "I will take care of it."

My throat felt dry and I could barely whisper. "How?"

"Tomorrow I will speak to the superintendent of the school and tell him I absolutely refuse to have you sent away."

"Won't that mean trouble for us?" Ursula wanted to know.

Mother firmly replied, "If we are to die, we will all die together and not leave one child under their influence alive and alone somewhere."

Other parents refused, too, so a few children were allowed to go to school every morning. An old, retired schoolteacher gave us a bunch of homework to do. We brought it back the next day, and he gave us some more. He never corrected it, or really taught us anything. So my last year of school really wasn't school at all.

I was lonely for Father, Horst, and Arno. I missed Leipzig and the happy days of my childhood. I was tired of war, Nazis, hunger, pain, air raids, angry people, and seeing my Mother so worried that she couldn't eat. It had been a long time since I had been truly happy. I wondered if I ever would be again. I couldn't remember when I last wished the war would end. Maybe I had lost hope.

CHAPTER 4

"Esther, are you ready yet?" I yelled impatiently, as I stood by the front door. I had begun tapping my brown loafer up and down in an attempt to release some of my pent up energy. It wasn't because I was worried that we would be late—we usually made up for lost time by running to the subway station—but I was ready to go and was getting tired of waiting for her as usual. Esther was much more concerned with her appearance than I. Even though I was now fourteen, I didn't take as long as my sisters to get ready for work.

"Karola, if you would let me fix your hair a few times, you would see how long it takes to get it just right," the voice from the bathroom explained.

"I can't let you—you take too long on your own hair," I retorted. Besides, I felt that my brown hair, with a soft touch of natural curl, didn't need much help. It suited me fine, and if others didn't like it, they didn't have to look at me.

"The people in our office building notice that you don't take the time like I do."

"The people in the office aren't worried about how a fourteen-year-old office apprentice fixes her hair."

The bathroom door swung open and Esther emerged. She held her head high, mimicking the behavior of a princess as she swept past me. I had to admit to myself that her attempt to beautify herself had paid off. The white collar on her light-blue cotton dress set off her dark, arched eyebrows. Her oval face was perfectly framed by her hair, and I knew that the workers in our office building would feel a rush of envy the moment Esther walked through the main entrance. I knew I was more of Esther's shadow than another worker to them; but I also knew Esther would pull me up beside her, put her loving arm around my skinny shoulders, and make me feel that I was just as beautiful as she.

I felt delighted to work with Esther in the same office building. When the sirens sounded during the day, it was comforting to find Esther and not have to face the danger alone. While some of the office workers crouched on the floor, suffering their distress in a crowd of people they barely knew, Esther and I talked and laughed together as if we were at a slumber party. I even saw some of the office workers glare at us as if we were breaking some unwritten rule, like, "Thou shalt not be joyful in an air raid shelter."

It was July of 1944. The sky was a misty gray-blue, the sun was warm, and the days were long. Green leaves on the trees on some of the larger, more industrialized streets provided color to satisfy our eyes, which were starving for shades other than the black and gray of ruins and rubble. Our lives were still in shambles, but having a routine helped to give us some consistency. I felt as if there was a reason for waking up each morning, other than running around frantically like a blind field mouse.

The smoke from last night's fires still hung in the air. On our way to work we passed several charred, crumbling skeletons of former buildings, but I wasn't bothered like I used to be. Some buildings had only a single outer wall left standing. We could look right through the windows and see pale blue sky or the apartment houses on the next block. Other buildings had the outer walls sheered completely off and we could see into people's apartments. Their furniture was covered with broken glass and plaster, but everything was left where it had been when the sirens sounded. Some of the apartments we passed were only half-apartments. Part of the building was intact; the other part totally demolished.

The scenery of Berlin had indeed changed since the Allies had begun stepping up the bombing in February; but the city's rush, rush, rush never seemed to change. Esther and I fit right in with the crowds covering the streets as we ran towards the subway station. Many stations were underground, but our station was up one flight of stairs. As we neared the station, we could see the train coming. Knowing that we had only thirty seconds before it left again, we sped up the stairs as fast as we could run.

The stationmaster stood in his dark blue uniform with a matching dark blue hat watching for us. He smiled when he saw us approaching. As usual, everyone was already on the subway and had found a seat when we came charging up.

"Just pay in the evening!" he called, waving us on.

We waved back, too out of breath to say anything. We ran onto the subway as it lurched forward towards the next station. Esther and I settled in a seat together and tried to stop panting.

"My glasses don't help me as much as they used to," Esther said, peeping over the rim of her glasses when her breath had slowed enough to allow her to talk.

I chuckled to myself. All that time she spent beautifying in the bathroom, and when we're out with people she peers over her glasses like a strange old woman. I noticed the mother in the seat in front of us trying to stop her two children from pointing at the "funny" lady.

"Maybe your glasses will work better," she said, snatching them from my face with little care.

"If you're not careful, my glasses won't help me like they used to." I took her glasses in a similar fashion, and we compared vision.

"No wonder you play so out-of-tune," I teased. "I can't see a thing with these."

"Yes," Esther solemnly nodded, "and these explain why you're singing is so off-key." I snatched at my glasses, but she held them out of reach. Suddenly I didn't care that people were staring, some astonished, others with understanding, still others with an envious flicker in their eyes. All I cared about at that moment was that I was playing with my sister. We were teasing and laughing and telling each other by our gestures and twinkling eyes that we loved one another very much. I knew that the love we felt had sustained me and kept me sane during this bitter, hateful war.

After riding the subway past three stations, Esther and I went to the door and hopped off before the train had completely stopped at the next station. We had only half a city block to walk to our destination.

When we reached the office building, we slipped through the front doors still laughing, but instead of our voices blending with the usual hum of noise, we were met with total silence. Not wishing to draw attention to ourselves, we, too, fell quiet.

I thought that some strange event must have happened in the war, but I couldn't be sure. Since we didn't have a radio, we didn't learn any news until we saw a newspaper. Sometimes the accounts we read about were already old news to the fortunate Berliners who had access to radios.

I drew Esther aside before she left for her own department. "Try to find out what's going on and then let me know."

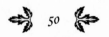

She nodded gravely. "Remember, Karola, we could be in serious trouble if we show joy for 'bad' news."

"Yes," I softly said. I knew what she meant. If the Nazis were losing the war and I behaved in a jubilant manner, it could cause the whole family a trip to a concentration camp if the wrong kind of people should see me.

I quietly went to my desk, keeping my eyes and ears attentive. Looking around the room at my co-workers, I wondered what they were thinking behind the scowls that showed on their faces. I was so busy studying them that I didn't see my desk clearly and as I awkwardly slid into my seat, I gouged my thigh on the pointed corner of my desk. The sharp pain made me angry at my clumsiness until I realized that I now held the same sour expression as my fellow workers; for once I fit right in.

It was difficult to concentrate on my work and listen to any conversations my co-workers dared have, but I was aching to know what was going on. The waiting was upsetting, and it seemed no one wanted to talk. A distinct hush lay over the office, as if someone had just carefully placed a blanket over another one of the war's many victims.

I had always been a person full of things to say, and I couldn't bear the silence around me. The only sound was the steady tap, tap, tap of the black typewriters. I hated sitting at my typewriter, not daring to speak to anyone, but I had to be careful. I suspected, but never knew, who was a Nazi spy.

This isn't right, I thought. *I'm just becoming a young lady; I should be happy and eager to talk and make new friends. It's all wrong; it's all Hitler's fault.* Hitler! The very name made me feel as if someone had poured icy water over my head during the middle of a hot day.

It was midway through the morning before I finally obtained the answer I sought. One of the ladies whom I worked with began whispering to another. When the word *assassination* came up in their conversation, I strained all the harder to hear.

"I tell you, someone tried to assassinate the Fuhrer."

"I thought that he was assassinated."

"Is he dead then?" asked the first lady.

"Well, I heard . . ." she quit talking and looked at me.

I suddenly realized that I had stopped my typing and she had noticed that I was listening. I quickly removed my glasses to wipe them with my handkerchief, but in my haste, I clumsily knocked them onto my desktop. The loud clank brought up the eyes of several workers close by. I nervously picked them up, shushing them under my breath. When I put them back on, I continued plucking intently on my typewriter. My chance to hear what had happened was destroyed. I didn't dare look at any co-workers or ask if the assassination was successful.

At my first break, I went to the rest room and combed my hair. Esther and I usually talked together at break time. I tried to appear casual while waiting for her to come.

"She may think it is better for us not to be seen together today," I told the pale green walls when too many minutes had ticked by. I put my comb away and started for the door.

"Karola, have you heard?" said Esther, coming into the rest room.

I got on my tiptoes to look past her in the hallway and check if anyone was nearby. No one seemed to notice us, so I took Esther's arm and pulled her into the rest room.

"I heard someone attempted an assassination," I whispered.

Esther straightened the white collar on her dress as a co-worker opened the rest room door. I fiddled with a loose string on my skirt and combed my hair again.

After the lady had gone, Esther said, "Well, I think that it wasn't successful."

I felt as if my heart had dropped with a definite thud to my shoes. "What makes you say that?" I nearly whimpered.

She looked around quickly and then whispered, "He must be alive because everyone still has a sober face."

"That's true," I nodded. "Surely there would be some happy faces if he were dead."

"Karola!" Esther gasped. "Be careful of what you say!"

"I will," I said matter-of-factly as I turned to go. "You be careful, too."

After work, while we were walking home from the subway station, I noticed a crumpled up newspaper in a wire basket by a bombed-out building. I reached into the basket and retrieved the paper. Esther and I huddled together in the broken doorway of what appeared to have been some sort of bakery. We discovered that we were right. Hitler was not hurt, but he swore revenge on everyone who had been involved in the attempt in any way. He declared "Total War" on all enemies.

"I wonder if Mother has heard?" I asked.

Esther shook her head. "I doubt it." She carefully folded the dingy, crinkled paper. "We should hurry and show her this."

We walked quickly, not daring to run and thus draw attention to ourselves. On a day like that day one couldn't be too careful. I entered the apartment with Esther close behind me.

"Mutter!" I called, looking quickly around. The quiet room was vacant.

"Mutter!" I called again.

"In the kitchen," a tired voice replied.

"Mutter, did you hear what happened?" asked Esther, holding the newspaper out to her.

Mother dabbed at her forehead with the back of one hand and took the paper with the other. We allowed Mother a few quiet minutes to read the headlines. When she had finished, she slowly shook her head.

"What does he mean, 'Total War'?" I asked, dreading the answer.

"Oh, Karola. You can guess, can't you?" Esther asked in scolding tones. "He means that no one is safe any longer."

"All civilians are to be regarded as soldiers, and all targets, military or not, are open to attack," Mother explained. Her tired sunken eyes looked down at the yellow newspaper in her hands.

She's hiding her fear from us, I thought. Poor, brave Mother, always trying to spare us the pain she feels. Yet, I could tell that she knew she must not hide the true world from us. She wanted us to know the ugly truth behind selfishness and let us see, first-hand, the pain it causes.

"If he does that to them, then they'll . . ." I stopped. Of course, they already knew. If Hitler treated civilians as soldiers and attacked any target, the Allies would do the same. Esther and I, and Edith and Ursula could be killed in our work places, even if they weren't military targets. We truly were living in a battle zone.

As the weeks went by we saw that Hitler's promise was being kept. Every civilian was treated like a soldier.

We hardly went to work anymore. The air raids were simply too heavy. The monster I had dreamed about long ago grew ten-fold and was a vivid part of this beastly nightmare.

Everything we did now was disrupted by air raids. From 10 A.M. until 12 noon we sat in the basement. Then again from 2 P.M. to 4 P.M., and again from 10 P.M. until midnight. Sometimes in the early morning the Russians flew over with observation planes and we again met our neighbors in the basement at 2 A.M.

When one squadron of planes left, the next one started. On the ground there was little left standing. Whole city blocks were literally eradicated, turned to black ashes and gray rubble.

People living in the center of the destruction area didn't stand a chance of getting out alive. Only those who lived on the edges could flee for their lives, leaving everything behind. The war had put on a new face, uglier than anyone had imagined. How, I wondered, could greed do this? Lives of countless individuals were disrupted, deteriorated, and destroyed. Because of one man's greed, indescribably horrible scenes were being played out everywhere. Bombs reduced beautiful architecture to debris, fire devoured anything salvageable, and people were left maimed and scarred at almost every street corner.

CHAPTER 5

The sirens had started again. I was instantly and completely awake and swiftly slipped the skirt that was lying on my bed over my head; my blouse and stockings were already on. I swung my legs to the floor and slipped my feet into my shoes. As I stood up, I zipped up the back of my skirt. The whole process took about seven seconds.

My suitcase and those of my sisters were packed and waiting by our bedsides. They contained extra clothes, genealogy, identification, ration cards, personal necessities—everything we could think of that we might require should our home be demolished and we need time to resettle somewhere else.

We gathered at the front door of our apartment, suitcases and extra blankets in hand, waiting for Mother. Her age, lack of food, and fatigue made her take a few seconds longer than my sisters and I. When she appeared, I opened the front door and started down the dark hallway to the basement.

"No, Karola!"

The squeal in Mother's voice stopped me and had the same effect as the first siren I'd ever heard. Chills sped down my spine, my hair prickled, and I turned around slowly to face the ghostly figure Mother had become.

"We're not going to our basement; we're going to the public shelter," Mother told us in a raspy voice.

I stared at her totally dumbfounded.

"But that takes eight minutes to get to," Ursula gasped, holding eight fingers up to stress her point.

"That's if we run," Edith added with a nod.

"Mutter," Esther said calmly, "we have only five minutes from the time the sirens start."

"Then get going, quickly!" Mother cried fearfully, shooing us ahead in the same way a street merchant would shoo a herd of hungry little children away from his table.

My sisters pushed past me, anxious to be off. As I listened to their feet quickly clamoring down the stairs, I wondered if they had noticed Mother's face. Her look had made my eerie feelings grow.

"Schnell, schnell Karola!" Mother cried, nudging me to go ahead of her.

"I'll help you," I offered, hooking my arm through hers. We stumbled down the four stories to the apartment building's main entrance. Only two minutes remained until the bombs would start falling, and we had eight minutes of running time ahead of us.

Mother hurried as best she could, but even for a healthy young person, the going was strenuous. All of the street lamps were off, and no light came through apartment windows. Even if a light had been on, we couldn't have seen it since everyone covered their windows for a total blackout condition. It was supposed to make it difficult for the enemy to hit their mark, but obviously it didn't help as much as we hoped.

Had it already been two minutes? I wondered as I heard the rumble of engines from the first squadron of planes. Between us and the death machines was only the helpless open sky. The hair on the back of my neck rose as the familiar whistle filled the air and the planes began carelessly dropping their bombs.

As each bomb exploded, the sky lit up brilliantly, making it easy to see debris and craters in the street. *That's one good thing,* I thought, not really noticing the irony. When it was dark again we were momentarily blinded, groping through the darkness; then, just as our eyes adjusted, another bomb exploded. We had to memorize the outlay of the craters and refuse in the street when the light exploded so that we could pass through when darkness surrounded us.

The public shelter we raced towards didn't provide me with any feelings of security. In fact, I felt it was extremely unsafe, and I didn't wish to end my life there. It was simply a tunnel dug underneath a railroad, reinforced with cement. A pungent smell came from a built-in outhouse that was treated with chemicals to help drive the stench away. The floor was also cement and put a damper on any thoughts I had entertained of trying to catch a little sleep during the air raid.

My sisters had arrived at the shelter before Mother and I, and they helped me guide her shaking, shallow form past the many people whose legs stretched out on the floor in front of them. We sat down when we came to the place my sisters had reserved for us and I noticed that beads of sweat were trickling down Mother's ashen face. It must have been terribly exhausting for a woman in her condition to run for her life through the streets of Berlin.

I kept telling myself that just a few minutes more would pass and then my nostrils wouldn't burn with the offensive smell. When I looked back at Mother, her jaw muscles were tightly clinched. I guessed it was against the odor but I wasn't sure. Again I wondered why she had asked us to come here.

She didn't seem to feel the sweat streaming down her face, so I fumbled through my skirt pocket for a handkerchief and wiped her forehead, cheeks, and neck. At last her eyes closed and she seemed to settle, resting her head on Edith's shoulder. Watching her, I silently prayed that she would be able to recapture some of the sleep that had eluded her so often.

Her rapid breathing gradually slowed, her jaw muscles relaxed, and it appeared that sleep was indeed coming to rescue her worn-out body. I suppose I studied her drifting off, because I needed to know she would be all right until I returned to her side. Moving from my spot on the cold floor, I crawled over bags of belongings, suitcases, and makeshift bedding until I was next to Esther. We were safely out of Mother's hearing if we kept our voices low.

Esther sat on the floor, resting her head on her rolled-up, yellow-green blanket. Her eyes were closed as if she were asleep, but I knew she wasn't.

"Esther, do you notice anything different about Mutter?" I whispered, gently shaking her shoulder in the hope that she would open her eyes.

Esther glanced quickly in Mother's direction and decided it was safe to respond. "She's got something against our shelter."

I nodded and was just about to say, "She seems afraid," when Esther continued. "Maybe something will happen there tonight."

I considered this for a moment before replying, "I don't think so. I got a good look at her—she's terribly afraid. She's never acted like that before. Even when the bombs were very close she was always so faithful and strong."

Esther was quiet. When she didn't reply, I said, "I'm going to ask Edith and Ursula what they think."

I crawled back to my spot and saw that Mother still seemed to be asleep. I felt it was safe to talk to Edith now, even with Mother resting on her shoulder. Mother probably wouldn't awaken for quite a while.

Edith was also resting her head against a blanket she had rolled up.

"Edith?" I whispered.

She quickly brought a finger to her lips, gesturing me to be quiet.

"What's the matter with Mutter?" I asked in a voice that was barely audible.

Edith shook her head ever so slightly. I sighed impatiently. What was that supposed to mean—she didn't notice anything, or she didn't want to talk about it? I ventured on.

"What should we do?"

Edith pressed her lips into a stern line. I knew I had upset her. Edith rarely got angry or impatient, but when it came to Mother she was very defensive. I was almost sorry for my inquiry, yet I felt I had to know. Any security I felt came from Mother, and if something was wrong with her, I was sure I wouldn't be able to continue.

Edith watched me as these thoughts hurried through my mind. She seemed to soften as she looked at me. Perhaps she understood that since I was the youngest child I needed the assurance that all was well with Mother. She tenderly touched my cheek with the back of her hand and smiled.

"We'll watch her closely," she spoke soft and slow. "Let's see if something really has changed."

A quiet peace encircled me and I nodded my head in reply. I was glad to know that if there were a problem, we would all face it together. My suitcase lay where I had dropped it, and I quietly retrieved my dark-blue cotton blanket, rolled it into a pillow behind my head, and closed my eyes.

As the days passed we noticed that a change had indeed taken place in Mother. Instead of being calm and faithful and trusting in the Lord, she was unusually panicky.

She still insisted that our basement wasn't safe enough. We

went to bed fully dressed so that at a moment's notice we could be on our way to the public shelter. Although we were no longer amateurs at experiencing air raids, we still ran the last three minutes to the shelter while bombs sounded their eerie warning whistle to their targets.

One evening between air raids we sat in the living room busying ourselves with darning, mending, reading, and anything else to pass the time. As I looked around the room at the faces of my cherished family, I became more and more determined to talk about Mother's problem. Surely this could not be allowed to go on. Someone would most likely be hurt if the problem weren't solved.

I remembered how Mother had told us of a woman in one of the apartment buildings who was always so afraid. She was afraid of the bombs, of starvation, of exposure, of soldiers, fire, and death. She had died just a short while ago. Strangely, the thing that had finally taken her life had not been any of the things she so greatly feared. She had just had a bath and, while stepping from the tub, slipped on a bar of soap and hit her head.

We had all reflected on the irony of this situation and decided that you just shouldn't live in such fear of everything. Yet, there was Mother. Lately she was behaving more like the paranoid woman than the pillar of spiritual strength and faith she had always been.

As I sat and darned my stockings, I watched Mother's head slowly fall back to rest on the back of the sofa. When I was certain she had fallen asleep, I motioned for Edith, Ursula, and Esther to follow me to the bedroom.

"What is it, Karola?" Ursula asked as I softly closed the door behind her.

"What are we going to do about Mother?" I put the question we all carried out in the open where we could thoroughly examine it.

The silence was complete. Everyone either looked down or nervously fumbled with their hair or hands. I knew none of us felt like we should tell Mother to do anything. We didn't feel it was our place.

Finally, Edith assumed her position as eldest and said in an authoritative way, "I think that the best thing to do is go along with what she wants."

I looked at her, startled.

"It may take her fear away," she explained, holding her hands out in a helpless sort of gesture.

"It may also make it worse," I retorted. "Look, since the Allies have come closer to Berlin, we have even less time to get to that shelter."

"I think we need to talk to her," Esther said.

I nodded in agreement.

Ursula looked at Edith, who thoughtfully studied her folded arms.

"When?" she asked, looking up.

"Why not right now, before the next air raid starts?" I suggested.

Edith let out a heavy sigh. "Well, I suppose it would be best," she doubtfully agreed.

I followed my sisters into the living room and was surprised to see Mother sitting in her favorite chair. I hoped she hadn't heard any of our conversation or wondered what we were doing. As I studied her I could tell that she hadn't done either. By the look on her face, the fear that now controlled her heart must have kept her from a restful nap.

Dark circles ringed her eyes, her weight had steadily dropped again, and her hair had changed to another shade of gray. I wondered if Father or Horst would recognize her if they were to walk through the door at that instant.

We knelt at her feet, and Edith took her hand and tenderly

caressed it for a moment before saying, "Mutter, we need to talk to you."

Mother responded to the gentleness in Edith's voice. The faraway look in her eyes faded and she focused fully on Edith's petite frame.

"Mother," Edith began, "we've noticed that you are very frightened. You seem to have even lost your faith in the Lord if that is possible."

Mother looked down, slowly shaking her head. "I am very much afraid," she said, her voice breaking with a sob. "This war is so terrible and ugly. I fear for your safety. I'm your mother; if anything happened to any one of you . . ." her voice trailed off as tears rolled softly down her cheeks, and she brushed them away slowly, her hand quivering.

Witnessing dear Mother's weakness was more than I could bear. I had always been able to stand any situation as long as she was all right, but seeing her so very tormented tore my heart into tiny, agonized pieces. I reached out for Esther's hand to help ease the pain I was feeling. Instead of holding my hand, she wrapped me in her arms, as if trying to protect me from my own anguish.

Edith rubbed Mother's hand to soothe her. "We understand that you are frightened, Mother, but is running around wildly looking for a different shelter really the answer you seek?"

Mother looked up, somewhat surprised, as if Edith had just told her something she had never considered. She was like a terrified child who has no place to turn to—not at all the steadfast, fearless woman she had been.

"Mother," I said, my voice sounding like a whimper, "the Lord has helped you through every trial in your life. Surely he can help with this one."

A gleam that I had seen long ago fought its way to Mother's eyes.

"Have you asked him for help?" asked Ursula.

"No," Mother replied, dropping her head sadly. We all waited. I looked at my sisters and knew the worried look I saw was reflected in my eyes as well.

Finally Mother raised her head. "You girls are right," she said. "I will pray and fast so that the Lord will help me get over my fear."

I sighed in relief. I knew the Lord would not deny her if she asked. I wanted her to be strong like she used to be. I needed her strength to support my own faltering faith. Each of us in turn bent and kissed Mother on her wrinkled cheek. After I did so, Esther again encircled me in her loving arms.

"We'll pray for you, too," Edith offered, rising to her feet.

"Oh, my good children," Mother softly said. "I do need your prayers. I would like that very much."

The next Sunday was a special meeting of the district of Berlin. The older I got, the more I enjoyed such meetings. This meeting was a spiritual feast. More and more, Sundays seemed to sustain me through the rest of the week. By week's end, I desperately needed to go to church. At last I felt like I knew what it meant to sup with the Lord.

On the way home I sat pondering the things I had heard as we rode the rapid subway called the S-Bahn. When we came to our station, the conductor went to each compartment and told everyone that an air raid had just begun.

"Go to the nearest bomb shelter," he instructed.

"We're just a short way from home," said Mother, turning to us. "Let's all hold hands and run to our own shelter."

Mother took Edith and Ursula's hands, Esther took Ursula's and my hand, and we began running toward home.

It was thrilling to run through the deserted streets, the wind numbing our ears and tossing our hair about in untidy waves. I could feel Esther's hand pulsing in mine as we ran. I glanced quickly at Mother to see how she was holding up.

Her face was radiant and her eyes shone.

"Girls!" Mother cried. "Stop!"

We all stopped, breathlessly looking at Mother.

"The bombs will not fall in our part of the city tonight." She began walking slowly, still holding hands as she explained, "They will fall over there, and there, and there." She released Edith's hand and pointed to three distinct areas.

We girls looked at each other and without saying a word, solemnly continued the walk home. A few minutes later, the bombs started falling. We could hear them whistle as they fell to their targets, but we calmly walked on with our steadfast Mother beside us.

After the raid was over, we went to the roof of our apartment building. Edith opened the door, and for a moment I remembered the many times I had come bursting through that same door as a nine- and ten-year-old child, playing games around Mother as she hung up the family wash. Was that really me, so carefree and happy? Did I once, only a few years ago, really live a life without fear?

It was a beautiful night. The sky was a dark, clear blue. The stars twinkled brilliantly. On the ground beneath us, just where Mother said there would be, were three big fires burning, marking the places where the bombs had fallen.

We stood staring, as though the scene before us was a fulfilled prophecy. Finally, I could stand it no longer. "I'm going down to ask Mother how she knew."

"Yes, how did she know, I wonder?" mused Esther.

We scrambled down the stairs. I've always been a fast runner, and I speedily left my sisters half a stairway behind me. I crashed through the door and found Mother carelessly resting in her favorite green chair. She hardly raised her head at my sudden thunderous intrusion.

"How did you know?" I blurted out.

A gentle smile crossed Mother's lips, and she waited for my sisters to catch up with me.

My sisters came through the door, and we stood in a row in front of Mother. Again I asked, "Mother, tell us, how did you know where the bombs would fall?"

"Girls," Mother began, sitting up straight in her chair, "from now on I will not be afraid." She paused and we stood perfectly still, waiting for her to continue. She looked each one of us in the eyes. Her stare seemed to bore a hole right to the center of my soul. I felt as if nothing could hide from her examining eyes. I had never experienced anything like it before. I knew with a burning sureness that she had received an answer to her prayers. What she was about to say had come from the Lord.

"The Lord took the veil off my eyes for just a split second." Her voice became stronger as she continued, "I saw the angels of destruction taking their places. They guided the bombs to their destinations. Now I know, if we live or have to die, it will be in the Lord."

I leaped to her side, throwing my arms around her. This was the mother I longed to see!

My sisters joined me, and we sat rocking one another, laughing, and crying, and even singing at the same time. That was the end of the terrible fear that had plagued her. From then on she was calm and completely trusting in the Lord. The people in our basement bomb shelter also saw a change in her. It made me smile, during one air raid, when I overheard two women talking.

"I wonder if the bombs will come close today," said one.

"I'll show you how you can tell," said the other. "Look at Frau Hilbert. She knows."

"What?"

"I noticed it the other day. Frau Hilbert was a little agitated, and the bombs fell close that day. Then, just last night, I watched her again, and she was just fine. You know, the bombs didn't fall near us last night."

The first woman looked at Mother, and when she saw that Mother was again calm, she shook her head in amazement.

"What did I tell you?" said the other. "You watch, today the bombs will not come near us."

Softly chuckling, I turned and went to Mother's side. I thought about the way these very people had treated Mother when we first moved to Berlin. Because she was a Mormon, they even crossed the street on the other side to pass her, as if being in her presence might soil them. Now, she had become their measuring stick. If she was relaxed, they too could relax; if not, prepare for the worst. I couldn't help but wonder if this would change the way they treated her when the war was finally over. But, strangely, I already knew it wouldn't.

CHAPTER 6

As the summer of 1944 came to a close, we heard a lot about the destruction taking place in eastern Germany, where the Russians were taking over. Some of the refugees came through Berlin, but most were rerouted to the north. I guess we weren't supposed to know too much. Our news was controlled by the Nazis and was mostly misleading and obviously tampered with.

Although it was extremely dangerous to listen to foreign radio, some of our friends had radios and received news from BBC–London. We learned some facts from them. Their accounts weren't as shocking as the stories of rape, plunder, and murder the refugees told. The horror stories from the refugees were difficult to believe. They told of barbaric atrocities, even crucifixion of women and children by the Russian soldiers. Surely this couldn't be true—the stories were so savage, so unreal. How could anyone even imagine such horrible things? We decided that reality lay somewhere between the refugees' tales and the foreign radio information.

Even if stories had been exaggerated, the thought of the Russians invading Berlin was terrifying to us. The takeover and forward thrust of the Russians had been alarming; we feared they would be heading westward, and prayed that the Western powers would take the city first.

Living conditions were already pitiful, between bombing, starvation due to a very limited food supply, and all the other trouble we had suffered until then. If we had to endure a Communistic takeover as well, could we survive such a nightmare?

One evening I stood by our white kitchen stove stirring a pot of Mother's delicious homemade soup with a wooden spoon. I tried not to let my thoughts turn back to my happy childhood and the way things used to be before the war. Doing so always made the present that much harder to tolerate. But every now and then I allowed myself to wallow in self-pity because things had turned out so badly. I wondered what would have become of me had all this never happened. What if Hitler hadn't come to power and Father hadn't told the Nazis he would only serve Jesus Christ? Would things be better or worse?

I startled myself with my own answer, and the wooden spoon fell from my hand. Eternal consequences would be much worse for us if we hadn't stood up for our beliefs. If Hitler hadn't come to power we might never have had the opportunity to show the Lord how much we would endure because we loved him and would stand up for his gospel. Tears started in my eyes and I silently prayed, "Thank you, Lord. Now you know how much we love you." I smiled inwardly. "And oh," I quickly added, "Thank you for a father who stands up for the right."

I looked back at the soup and my thoughts continued to flow around my family. I missed Horst, Father, and Arno terribly. Father's company was still in Thuringen. He visited us occasionally, but his visits were fewer and further apart, depending on the air raids. Since Hitler's assassination attempt, Father hardly came to visit us at all.

We had received news that Arno had been wounded in Russia and had been taken to the Italian front, which meant that he was probably in an American prison by now. Actually that was good news. An American prison was much preferred over a Russian one. However, a prisoner is still a prisoner.

I longed for more news of Horst, no matter how awful. We had been notified by the German Army that he had been wounded in Russia. A grenade had exploded close by him and shrapnel covered the entire left side of his body. In spite of his trouble, his letters were always filled with humorous anecdotes. I knew it was his way of trying not to show his misery in order for us not to worry about him.

I slowly stirred the soup. The steam and aroma drifted up to my nostrils and caused my stomach to grumble impatiently. The soup was ready, and I couldn't wait another second. "Dinner's ready," I called.

"Edith isn't here yet," said Ursula from the living room. She was using black thread to mend a tear in a brown skirt and being as careful as she could so that the black thread wouldn't show through. We were out of brown thread and there was no way of knowing when any would be available again.

I went to the window to look for Edith. Being hungry made me terribly impatient about having meals on time. Looking down at the street, my thoughts drifted again to my childhood and the times Esther and I had been sent to look out the window to keep us entertained.

In a way, the scene hadn't changed much. There were still people busily hurrying up and down the street, hardly noticing others when they passed by, anxious to get to some destination. Yet, in another way, the scene had changed dramatically. Now the people sidestepped craters and debris. Though I couldn't see details clearly from the fourth floor, I knew that the clothes they wore had been made over again and again. Everyone made do with what they had.

The scene depressed me, and I was just about to turn away

when I saw Edith coming toward our apartment house.

I waited until Edith burst through the front door before announcing again, "Dinner's ready!"

"Yes, we can eat now. Edith's here," Esther cried, jumping up from the piano bench where she had been lost in another world thanks to the music of Bach. Mother rose from the sofa where she had been crocheting a scarf with several colors of leftover yarn.

We quickly sat up to our places, the pleasant aroma filling the air and making my mouth water. My stomach growled audibly, but no one embarrassed me by mentioning it.

Mother usually waited until we had settled around the table before calling on someone to bless the food. Instead, this time, she took an envelope from her pocket.

"I was waiting for everyone to be home so I could read this letter to you," she told us.

We all started talking at once.

"Who's it from?"

"Where's it from?"

"Did you open it?"

"What does it say?"

"Is it from Horst?"

Mother held her hand up for silence and opened the letter. "It's from Poland," she said. "Hush now, let me read."

Liebe Familie,

Do you remember when I was wounded in Russia? Shrapnel from a grenade covered half of my body and the field doctor took a piece from my neck with no anesthetic. I got even as best I could by calling him a . . .

Mother's face reddened as we girls exchanged twinkling

glances and she cleared her throat. "Anyway, you don't need to hear that part of his letter," she said. "Now, let's see . . ."

Now that I have recovered, you would think that the Army would send me to the front again. But no, they must keep us confused and guessing. Therefore they sent me to Poland where I am training the grandfathers of Germany! Why, you ask? Well, I will explain. When I had recovered, the officials noticed my handsome physique, and decided that I could instruct the German men (ha, ha). I was sent to Poland and am training WWI veterans for combat.

Karola, remember the day I went to war and we laughed about how hard it would be for Father to spank me if I were old? Well, it's not so far from the truth. All the men could be my father and it's hard for me to tell them what to do. I really hate training them, since many of them are even older than Father. However I am thankful not to have to fight anymore.

Lovingly, your son and brother,

Horst

Thinking of the day when Horst went to war made me want to laugh and cry at the same time. "I remember what Horst said the day he went away. I couldn't stop laughing long enough to catch a breath," I reminisced aloud.

"Dear Horst, he didn't know when to stop. I always feared for you when he started telling jokes," Mother told me. "He couldn't stop joking, even when you laughed so hard your face turned blue."

"And now he is in Poland. Well, like he says, at least he's not fighting," Edith added.

Mother's face showed relief. I knew she had been worrying

and praying for Horst continuously. "Well, it's good to get some news from him. Now we can put our thoughts to rest," Mother said as she folded the letter and placed it carefully back into the envelope.

"Let's eat then," I said, rubbing my hands together in anticipation.

"Yes, offer the prayer, Karola. And remember to thank the Lord that Horst is no longer in the fighting zone."

I did as I was told, but even after I said amen I continued to thank the Lord. With every spoonful of delicious soup I raised to my mouth, I thanked him that Horst was alive and didn't have to fight.

❀ ❀

Fall arrived in its usual way, bringing a cutting chill to the air. Rust-red leaves riding the wind twisted and twirled together in a merry dance as they took their journey to the sidewalks and roads.

Esther and I tried to walk more briskly to work in order to force our blood to pump faster and fight the wind chill. Most of the time this helped, but we still arrived at the office building with red noses and ears that hurt from the cold.

One nippy evening a quick knock sounded on our door. It was nearly dinnertime, and I selfishly hoped it wasn't anyone who would be staying to eat with us. But, when Ursula opened the door, I quickly swallowed my ugly wish in one guilty gulp.

"Horst! Meine gute!" I happily cried, running with my sisters to embrace him. Mother stayed in her chair, too weak to get up, even for this joyous surprise.

His laughter burst through the room, making the whole apartment seem to sway to its rhythm. He couldn't stop giggling, even when we'd finished welcoming him by ruffling his hair and pulling him around to the path we'd made for him to stand before Mother.

A deep chuckle started in Mother's throat as she looked at him. There he stood in full uniform, his hair in complete disarray, his shoulder strap crooked, his jacket unbuttoned, and his face red with glee.

"Horst," Mother burst out with a laugh, "I don't think you'll ever grow up."

Horst tenderly kissed her cheek. "I hope not," he replied.

"What are you doing here?" I asked.

Horst turned to me. "Why, my dear, I'm an important person. Almost as important as you."

I blushed, somewhat embarrassed that he didn't seem to notice I was becoming a young lady and that he shouldn't talk to me as if I were a child.

"I've come through Berlin on assignment."

"What kind of an assignment?" I asked.

"Getting away from the Russians," he explained.

Mother's face turned pale, but Horst quickly added, "It's all very official, so I can't say anymore."

There was an awkward silence, and then I remembered dinner. "I suppose the army never gave you rations for your trip, so you'll just have to eat with us."

"You read my mind," said Horst. "Or maybe it was my stomach?"

"I didn't have to read it—it sounds like you're carrying a whole battalion in there."

Horst laughed, and we all gathered around the table.

After dinner, before the air raids, we talked and Horst told jokes as only he could. It was good to see laughter on the faces of those I loved so dearly. But it seemed strange to laugh. My face was so unaccustomed to it that my cheeks ached until I had to rub them.

"Horst, stop!" I begged, trying desperately to hold my cheeks straight.

"Please don't be so funny!" Ursula added, rubbing her aching face.

Horst ignored our pleas and started another joke. But he didn't finish it—the shrill of air raid sirens interrupted him. We jumped up, grabbed our suitcases and extra blankets, and hurried to the basement.

The atmosphere in the basement changed with Horst there. He told the jokes he had just told us. Our neighbors were holding their sides and slapping their knees as their laughter drowned out the whistle of the bombs.

It lasted about two hours. The "all's clear" siren blew and we started gathering our things. Some of the neighbors shook Horst's hand, thanking him for the good time. Perhaps they felt as I did, as if a lively party had just come to an end.

We dragged our weary bodies up to our apartment. We were all tired and ready to go to bed. Edith opened the door, and we filed inside, setting our suitcases in a row by the door, ready for the next raid.

"Let's kneel for prayers," Mother said. The sound of fatigue in her voice made me stretch and yawn before collapsing on the floor beside Esther.

Mother waited until we all appeared to be ready, then she smiled at Horst. "Would you please offer prayer?"

I expected a quick, witty reply from him, but instead he seemed to soften; his eyes were moist and he solemnly bowed his head. The prayer that he offered made the hairs on my arms and legs stand. I never thought I would hear anyone but Mother and Father pray like that, but I was wrong. Horst did more than repeat some familiar sayings we had fallen into the habit of using; he pled with the Lord. He spoke reverently and respectfully as he begged our Father in Heaven to stretch out his arms and encircle us in love. He prayed for Father and Arno, Mother and us girls, his wife and her family. He prayed for peace and safety, and that we might have charity in our hearts toward everyone. At last he asked our Heavenly Father to answer our petition only if it was according to his holy mind and will.

The prayer ended, but no one moved. Peace had settled over our hearts, and it seemed that everyone thought—as I did—that if we moved, the delicate calm would leave. It felt so good to absorb the warmth it brought.

Mother held out her arms to us and we flocked to her, gently hugging her good night. All was well in our home for one more night. We girls kissed Horst without being playful and scurried off to bed.

Horst and Mother sat in the kitchen and talked while I slowly drifted off to sleep. Hearing his voice gave me the same feeling as sitting on Mother's lap in a rocking chair and having the gentle motion rock me to sleep.

I vaguely remember hearing Horst speak of plans he had made to escape to the West so he could be in an American prison. He had been with us for only a few hours and must be going.

Then his voice became very solemn. "Mother, you, too, must run to the West."

"Horst . . ." Mother began.

"Mother, listen," he interrupted. "You must do as I say. Take the girls and run to the West. The Russians are coming and I have seen what they will do."

Mother hesitated. "Horst, where could we go? The chances of being stuck on the highways to West Germany are so great!"

"You will get through," Horst reassured her.

"What if we were caught out in the open with nowhere to go and the Russian soldiers came? There would be no safety! No

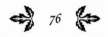

place to hide! No, we are wiser to stay where we are. We might have a better chance for protection right here."

"Mother, if the Russians come to Berlin it will be most terrible. I'm afraid for all of you." Horst stopped. I imagined he must have seen a determined look on Mother's face. "Well then, remember one thing," he continued. "Soldiers will go to the basement where they know everyone is hiding from the shootings. They are too lazy to climb stairs; besides, they are always in a hurry. Maybe this will help you to protect the girls."

"I will remember that," Mother said.

"I must go," said Horst.

I could hear him gather his things and pause at the door to hug Mother and tell her good-bye.

Hearing the door close was like hearing a casket shut. It seemed to have the same solemn finality. I sat up in bed. "Horst," I sobbed quietly.

I didn't think anyone had heard me, and then I saw Mother standing in the doorway.

"Go to sleep girls," she gently urged.

"Is Horst going to be okay?" I asked.

"If he can escape to the West he will be all right."

"What if he can't?"

There was a long pause before Mother finally answered, "We will put him in the hands of the Lord, Karola. That's all we can do now."

I quickly turned my face to my pillow and muffled my sobs until I fell asleep.

The winter of 1944–45 came and brought with it more misery and fear. The Western powers arrived at the Elbe River, about one hundred miles west of Berlin, while the Russians were at the Oder River, which was one hundred miles to the east. Dear Berlin was right in the middle, helpless, yet hopeful.

CHAPTER 7

Most of our days started with a two-hour air raid that lasted from ten o'clock till noon. For the rest of the day, all of our activities were sandwiched between air raids, and we spent much of our time in the basement. There just wasn't time to do many things, so at the office where Esther and I were apprenticed, less and less was accomplished. Sometimes we were asked to help fortify the area where we worked by sandbagging bridge entrances. Finally, there was no reason to go to work at all.

During this time, my fifteenth birthday drew near. I was looking forward to this birthday because, at fifteen, I would surely now be counted among the young ladies. I wanted to be more like my older sisters, whom I thought were truly ladylike. To top it all off, this year my birthday would fall on a Sunday. It appeared that a terrific day would at last materialize for me, even in spite of the sad war.

On Saturday, February 3, we had an extremely intense air raid. It started at 10 A.M. The planes stayed very close to the north of us and sounded as if they were only a few blocks away.

As usual, I started thinking about the people who were directly under the attack. I remembered a young mother, Sister Latschkowski, from our branch who lived in that area. She had three little boys—the oldest was five and the youngest was still a baby. I wondered how she would manage with her little ones if her apartment house were hit. The more I thought about her, the more uneasy I became. Visions of her struggling to save her children from fire began swarming in my mind. I paced back and forth, eager to go and see for myself if she needed our assistance.

The gray walls of the basement seemed like a prison. The screeching bombs outside held me in better than any bars could. Still, I was restless. The darning I brought with me to help pass the time lay untouched on my suitcase.

I knew that Edith would be all right at work since that part of the city wasn't under attack. I was glad for one person I didn't have to worry about during this particular raid. But what of the others? Was there anything worse than not knowing and waiting? It seemed all we did anymore was wait. Wait for news of the war, of Father, of Horst, of Arno; wait for sirens; wait for the "all's clear"; wait for the bombs to fall; wait to eat; wait to sleep; wait to bathe; wait, wait, wait! How could we wait when we knew someone needed us?

My shoes scratched the cement floor as I walked. Scrape, slide, scrape, slide—what an eerie sound they made.

"Oh, Karola," cried Ursula. "Stop doing that. It's making my skin crawl."

I stopped. Toe, heel, toe, heel. No sound at all came from my shoes. Heel, toe, heel, toe—that way the slightest little scratch accompanied the toe.

The loud blasting sound of the "all's clear" interrupted my lively feet. At last the air raid was over. I hurried to the twelve metal basement steps and started climbing them behind Ursula. As my shoes tapped the metal, my thoughts returned to Sister Latschkowski. I wondered if we could do anything for her. Part of me wanted to run and assist her, yet another part was hesitant, apprehensive about what I might find. Still, I had to know.

"Mother!" I turned so quickly that I nearly knocked her off balance.

"Karola," she said in a slow, scolding tone.

"Sorry," I awkwardly apologized.

"I wish I had your energy," she observed.

I waited until she was all the way up the basement steps and safe on the courtyard ground before asking, "Couldn't Esther and I go and . . ."

Mother cut me off with a wave of her hand as she tried to catch her breath. "I was just thinking," she said. "Someone ought to go to Sister Latschkowski's apartment and see if she's all right."

I smiled, delighted to see that for once I shared an inspiration with Mother. "That's what I was going to say," I blurted, relieved.

Mother looked up at me. "Go ahead then, and take Esther with you."

"Come on, Esther," I turned and called. She was already across the courtyard at the apartment house door. "Mother wants us to check on Sister Latschkowski."

Esther whirled around and hurried to my side. We left our apartment house together in a smooth, even trot.

After three blocks, destruction started. We jumped over the debris and craters in the road where we could still hear time bombs ticking. Occasionally a burning beam from a nearby apartment house would come crashing to the street and we would scramble out of the way, momentarily disoriented by a near miss with death.

When we reached Sister Latschkowski's apartment building, the front was an orange and black maze of fire, but it was still standing. We ran through the entrance, across the open courtyard, and toward the rear entrance.

What a chaotic scene met our eyes! The house around her was on fire and the walls were so hot the light green paint was blistering; yet she sat on the bed in total bewilderment, shaking her head, her hands turned upward on her lap in a helpless gesture. "What shall I do? What shall I do?" she sobbed again and again.

I went to her side. "Sister, listen. It's me, Karola Hilbert. You remember me?" I gently patted her shoulder while I tried to talk softly. I knew I must swallow down the disturbing sense of urgency I felt, for it could make me cruelly impatient, and then she might not respond to me at all. "You've got to leave. Where are your boys?"

"What shall I do, Karola?" she sobbed again. Her eyes held an empty look, as if her mind were slowly drifting away to some safe spot in her soul where bombs didn't tick and fires didn't burn.

"The baby's in his crib," Esther called out to me. I glanced in her direction and noticed that five-year-old Siegfried was helping her stuff clothing into a suitcase. She had pulled a baby carriage close by to use as a cart for carrying their belongings.

"Where's your other little boy?" I asked, shaking Sister Latschkowski's shoulder as gently as I could without becoming fierce. "You can't leave us now," I silently told her. She must remember where the boy was. Fear often led children to peculiar places to hide while fire destroyed their homes. Although rescuers searched desperately, too often their searching found nothing but bad news.

The shocked woman stared blankly at me for a moment, then she suddenly remembered. "Hospital," she said.

Anxiety slipped off of me like a loose shawl from chilled shoulders, and I allowed myself a brief moment to bask in the warmth of relief. Certainly her little boy, though ill, was better off in the hospital than here. And there he would be safe.

"We'll take your boys home to our mother." I spoke loudly, hoping my voice was getting through. "Shake the broken glass off your bed sheets and put your things in them. We'll be back," I instructed her. I rose from her side and helped Esther put baby blankets and clothes in the baby carriage, then the baby, and finally a loaded suitcase beside him.

"Come on, Siegfried," I urged. "Stay close to us." Esther and I dashed out the door with Siegfried, the baby, and the buggy. Esther pushed the buggy as far as the road would allow. "You're going to have to help me carry it," she finally said. "There's too much debris to push it home."

I grabbed the front and we somehow made our way, lifting and pushing the buggy and its precious contents home.

"Mother!" we called from the hallway outside our apartment. She opened the door just before we reached it.

"Please watch Siegfried and the baby," Esther gasped breathlessly.

"We need to help Sister Latschkowski," I explained. "Her apartment house is on fire!"

Mother had already taken Siegfried's hand and tried not to show her concern. I knew she was afraid of upsetting the little boy. She urged us to hurry with a "Yes, yes," and a nod of her head.

Ursula appeared at Mother's side. "Can I help?" she asked, a look of concern flooding her eyes.

"Yes, go on," Mother told her, stepping aside to let her pass. "Three of you will be able to save more of her things."

Ursula, Esther, and I ran right back to Sister Latschkowski's apartment. She hadn't moved.

"Come, come, Sister," Esther called to her. She and I each took one of her arms and moved her to the sofa; we needed the blankets and sheets from the bed. Ursula cleared the shattered glass and we three emptied the contents of dresser drawers onto Sister Latschkowski's bed. Ursula quickly tied the bundle in a secure knot and handed it to Esther. While she ran out, Ursula and I started on the next bundle.

"Sister, come help us," I urged. She looked at me and nodded her head. It appeared she was beginning to come around. Ursula went to her side and gently patted her arm, trying to help her return to the awful reality around us.

My lungs were screaming for air; I grabbed the bundle and ran outside. I trotted across the courtyard to the front of the apartment house, gulping fresh air gratefully. I dropped my bundle next to the one Esther left across the street, jogged back across the courtyard, and took a couple of deep breaths before diving back into the smoky ruins.

Esther took Sister Latschkowski outside for air while Ursula and I filled another sheet with clothes, food, and what few possessions we could find. When we ran out, Esther and Sister Latschkowski came back in. Sister Latschkowski was slow in her movements, but at last she seemed to be able to discern what was going on.

Eventually the smoke became so thick that when I opened the main entrance door to run through the courtyard toward her apartment, I couldn't see my hand in front of my eyes.

"It's no use going back anymore," Esther called from behind me. She and Sister Latschkowski were coming towards Ursula and me from across the street.

I could see that Esther was right. It was useless to try to save any more. The rest of the apartment house was falling down. Once a fire started, it just kept burning until there was nothing left to burn. We were helpless to do anything more.

I turned away from the dying building, which was creaking and groaning as if in pain, and followed Esther back to the street. We had saved many of Sister Latschkowski's belongings, yet not enough by far. We stood there surveying the damage. I was tired but pleased I had been able to help.

"There's not going to be much of a home left for us when that fire gets through," Sister Latschkowski stated quietly.

Hearing the resignation in her voice sent a familiar tightness to my chest.

Esther must have felt the same way. "You should come home with us," she told her.

"I'm sure we'll be able to resettle," Sister Latschkowski said hesitantly.

"Your children are already with Mother. Why don't you stay until you have somewhere to go?" Ursula asked.

"I suppose that's the only thing for me to do," she replied.

We each took a bundle and walked slowly away from the crackling building towards home.

Late that night the doorbell rang. Edith was trying to feed the baby and Esther and I fed Siegfried so that Sister Latschkowski could rest. Mother opened the door while we anxiously waited to see who it was.

"Mother Hilbert!" cried Irene, Horst's wife, with outstretched arms when the door opened. Her mother stood sheepishly behind her in the hallway.

"Meine gute!" Mother exclaimed. "Come in, come in."

Irene and her mother stepped in together while we bombarded them with questions.

"What's the matter?"

"Is Horst all right?"

"Is your apartment gone?"

Irene smiled gently at our concern. "Let me put my things down and take off my shawl, then I'll tell you what's happened."

"Yes, of course," Mother said, helping her with her suitcase

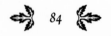

and shopping net that was full of extra clothes and a few cans of food.

"Come, sit down, Sister Buchta." Ursula got up from the sofa to offer Irene's mother her seat.

"Why, thank you." Sister Buchta smiled gratefully at Ursula.

"Our home is not lost," Irene reassured us, sitting down on the sofa by her mother. "But we have been advised to leave until the army can take care of some time bombs that are all around it."

I breathed a sigh of relief for them. At least their home was still standing. "I hope they can take care of the bombs before your home is destroyed," I said.

"Yes," Irene nodded, "we thought it best to stay with you tonight."

"You made the right choice," Mother consoled them. "Have you had anything to eat?"

"We couldn't take your food," said Sister Buchta forcefully.

"All that we have is yours," Mother generously offered.

Edith warmed some broth and gave Irene and her mother a bowl. We continued talking while they ate, and at last it was time for all of us to go to bed.

I slept on the floor in the living room with Esther, Ursula, and Edith. Irene, her mother, and Sister Latschkowski, along with her little boys, occupied our four beds.

I was the first to awaken. Perhaps I was still a little girl at heart and the expectation for my birthday had awakened me. How I wanted to stand up and shout, "Everyone get up! Sing to me! Bring me my presents! It's my birthday!" Instead, I quietly waited for the others to stir. I did need to act like I was fifteen, for Siegfried's sake at least.

The sound of a drawer softly closing in Mother's room made my stomach dance with excitement. I knew Mother would soon appear. Then, at long last, the birthday festivities would begin.

As soon as Mother began fixing breakfast, I sat up and watched her, but she didn't even glance at me. She seemed to be thoughtfully engaged in making sure we would have enough breakfast for everyone.

Esther was up next and went straight for the bathroom down the hall. Then Siegfried was running through the house, the baby was crying, Edith was scolding Esther for not folding her blankets before she left, and everyone was trying to get washed and dressed at the same time.

At breakfast I remained unusually quiet, watching my mother and sisters for the slightest hint that they had suddenly remembered; but they gave no indication that such was the case. They didn't even notice my glumness—there was too much commotion at the breakfast table. I wanted so desperately to remind them but I felt too proud. It just isn't a happy birthday if you have to announce it to everyone.

"I've decided that Edith, Ursula, and Esther should go to church to find out if everyone in the branch is all right," Mother was saying. "The rest of us can stay home to feed the baby and prepare enough food for everyone."

This news only increased my sadness. I was hoping that maybe at church someone might remember to wish me a happy birthday.

While I was preparing dinner in the kitchen with Mother, I noticed that quite often she seemed to be studying me over the rim of her glasses. I sensed she could tell something was wrong with me; however, I didn't say anything, and neither did she. Inwardly, I was glad that she noticed my quietness. At least she was finally thinking of me. Perhaps her thoughts would bring her to my birthday and it would be remembered after all.

Edith, Ursula, and Esther came from church with good news: no one else had been hurt. We all felt relieved.

We let our guests sit at the dining table with Mother, while we four girls ate at the kitchen table. We enjoyed our meal, especially having the baby and Siegfried there to watch. Esther would tease the poor baby until he stuck out his lower lip, ready to cry. Then Esther would laugh and laugh. She thought he looked so cute with his little "shovel," as she called it.

We cleared the table and Mother and I began washing dishes. She said we better wash them now or we wouldn't have any clean dishes left for our evening meal.

"Karola, you look at me so strangely. Have I done anything wrong?" she asked.

"Oh, no," I answered soberly, looking at the dishwater in the tub, and yet I felt so anxious for her to remember and celebrate my birthday with me.

That afternoon we gathered on the floor in the living room and played Hide the Button with Siegfried while Mother sat in her chair and Sister Buchta, Sister Latschkowski, and Irene sat on the sofa and talked.

Mother watched me thoughtfully out of the corner of her eye, when suddenly she sat up and clapped her hands. "I remember, Karola!" she exclaimed, her whole face lighting up. "Today is your birthday!"

My heart beat wildly with glee! A triumphant smile filled my whole being and parted my once sober lips.

"Oh yes!" Esther cried, jumping up from the floor. She held up her arms in a conductor's stance. "Everybody sing to Karola!" Even little Siegfried sang clearly and loudly. And with so many people, they produced a wonderful birthday chorus for me.

When the song ended, Edith smiled and said, "I've been saving something for you." She hurried off to the bedroom in a cheerfully mysterious way.

"That reminds me," said Esther, following Edith.

"I'll be right back," Ursula announced. Knowing their

absence would bring joy on my behalf quickly added to the suspense that had filled the apartment.

Moments later I had a lap full of tiny gifts wrapped in yellowing newspaper my sisters had kept hidden just for this occasion. Siegfried watched, almost as exuberant as I was. The little treasures I had collected for my birthday brought a monumental joy, and for that time the outside world was completely forgotten. I received hand-me-down stockings from Ursula, a calendar book from Edith, and a blouse of Esther's I had long admired.

The rest of the evening was spent playing games that I chose. Although I was now officially fifteen, I felt as happy as a four-year-old on Christmas morning. At last we had a merry birthday celebration.

Feelings of helplessness crowded over us in our seemingly endless situation. Day after day we sat in the basement listening to bombs crash and devastate the city. First we always heard a high-pitched whistle that grew louder and louder until it culminated in one terrible explosion. The closer the bombs fell, the louder they whistled. The ground shook with each crash, and our nostrils filled with the dusty plaster that sifted down from the ceiling.

Of course, if the bomb was very close, there was no whistle, only the unexpected violent explosion. Without warning we would be thrown into each other's arms or across the room.

During this period in our survival, we asked one special blessing from our Father in Heaven—that when the time came for our part of the city to be destroyed, somehow, we would not be there.

So far we rarely had air raids on Sundays. It seemed that we

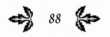

were allowed this one day to rest. On Sunday, March 18, 1945, while we were in church as usual, the Sunday School superintendent stood up and opened his mouth to greet the congregation. But the only sound that reached our ears was the penetrating screech of the dreaded sirens.

I watched my mother and sisters, and by the looks on their solemn faces I could tell their thoughts were the same as mine. We all knew without saying a word that this would be the day our neighborhood would be bombed. There wasn't any other time when all of us were gone away from home all together. I felt so grateful that the Lord had left the choice up to us. We could be either in his house on the Sabbath, or in our own.

The Sunday School superintendent was motioning everyone toward the door. I knew he was signaling us to run to the public air-raid shelter around the corner that was only two minutes away.

As we sat in the shelter, I began thinking of Sister Latschkowski. She had been able to take her three boys and move into an apartment at the back of our apartment house. This morning before church she stopped by to let us know she would be gone visiting a friend of hers who lived on the outskirts of Berlin. "Thank goodness she won't be under the bombs today," I thought.

I still remembered the way her home was slowly devoured by fire. The fire had looked like a ravenous orange tongue coming from windows and doorways, licking life from everything it touched until all was black and repulsive. I wondered if the same thing was happening to our home and our possessions. What about our neighbors in the basement? I hoped they had been able to hear the warning sirens.

When the "all's clear" siren sounded, we grimly looked at one another. Now the moment had come. Would we find our home left standing or would a total hit have reduced it to ruins?

Would fire be burning, hungry and uncontrolled, devouring everything worth saving? Would half our home remain intact, while the other half met destruction? Would the outside walls be shorn away, exposing our private little abode to curious eyes? The answer could only come if we left the shelter, but somehow I didn't want to go. I was afraid of what I might find.

"Quick, girls," Mother's voice penetrated my thoughts. "We must be off."

I stood up and helped Mother to her feet. Pulling her close to me, I suddenly felt strong. I could face anything if Mother was there.

"What if our home . . ." Esther began the question we all had in our minds, but Mother shook her head.

"We will see," was all she said.

We stepped into the open air and saw the ugly black smoke in home's direction swirling to the sky. The closer we came to our street, the more destruction there was. Fires were still burning, and people were rushing in and out, saving what they could.

For half an hour, we ran as fast as our feeble legs could go. For one brief moment I marveled at how the anxiety of not knowing what had happened seemed to feed energy to my tired muscles. Time bombs ticked away indifferently, hiding in craters in the street; fires devoured homes and debris; cries from frightened children rang out above the sounds of chaos; and, at last, our street corner came into view. A similar scene was displayed on our street, but I hardly noticed. All that my eyes took in was that our apartment building was still standing!

I began to cry—I couldn't stop myself. Tears I had kept in check while we waited in the shelter came spilling down my cheeks.

I rushed to Mother's side and hugged her, crying, "Oh Mother, it's there, it's there!"

Mother patted my head gently. "The Lord has been good to us once more," she said.

She's teaching me now, I thought to myself, and I looked up into her face. Her eyes searched mine for the clue she always sought that I had paid attention and had learned from an experience.

"I'm so grateful," I said. Yes, so grateful that he had watched over us again. Thankful that he had given me a mother who was always teaching, even in the face of turmoil.

Mother softly brushed my cheek with the back of her hand. "Let's see if everyone is all right."

I released my embrace and followed her down the metal steps to the basement. Mother was met by one of our neighbors, a short woman with stripes of gray through her red hair. She adjusted the blue smock on her shoulder and pointed at Mother.

"We knew it was today when we saw you weren't here," she said.

A puzzled look crossed Mother's face.

Our stocky neighbor explained, "When we came down to the basement and saw your usual corner empty, we started asking, 'Where are the Hilberts?' 'Why aren't the Hilberts here?' 'Have they gone?' Then someone said, 'It's Sunday—they are always in church on Sunday.' We were all very grim because we knew it would happen to us today. We felt sure!"

"How did our apartment building ever survive?" asked Mother.

"Oh," cried the woman, her eyes growing larger, "we were very fortunate. Two older men ran upstairs during a little pause in the bombing, since they felt certain that our building had been hit." She paused, licking her lips. I felt that she hoped the pause would add suspense to the story. But she didn't need to bother because the story was suspenseful enough without her added tactics.

"They were right!" she continued. "It was some of those phosphorus bombs that come down in bundles. They quickly picked them up with a shovel and threw them out the attic window to the street. Then they took the sand from the barrels and smothered the fire that started."

"What a brave thing for them to do!" Mother exclaimed.

"Yes, they are our heroes!" the woman cried ecstatically.

"Everyone is all right then?" Mother asked, looking around the room.

"Oh, yes! And our apartments are intact."

"Wonderful!" Mother exclaimed, clapping her hands. Turning to us girls she said, "Well, come then, there's nothing for us to do here."

We followed her in single file back to our apartment. I could tell that she was in a thoughtful mood. As soon as we had entered the door, she said, "Girls, I want you to come and kneel in a circle." She made a circular motion with her thin hands to help urge us to our prayer positions.

We quickly obeyed, leaving our sweaters wrapped around us rather than hanging them up on the hooks by the door like we usually did when we entered our apartment.

Mother slowly looked at each one of us. "I hope you understand what has happened today. We have prayed long and hard to our Heavenly Father that we would not be home when our part of the city was destroyed. Today, it was, and where were we?"

She waited for an answer. I quietly supplied one: "At church."

"Yes," she said, nodding. "We could choose to be in church or home. I'm so thankful that we all chose to be where we are commanded to be on the Sabbath day."

We knelt there quietly, each with her own thoughts. I suppose at that time I didn't fully realize just how blessed we had been. After a long pause, Mother said, "Let us thank our Father in Heaven for his watchful care."

We reverently bowed our heads and Mother offered a prayer of thanks. As she prayed, the thought occurred to me that Mother prayed for everything. Not only did she remember other people in her prayers, but she always remembered to thank the Lord for his mercy and vigilance.

I remembered being very tired and sore from kneeling so long during Mother's prayers as a child. My brother Arno used to say that listening to Mother pray was like riding the subway. Far, far away you could see the end station and as the train approached, it gradually got slower and slower, and then went right through it without stopping. I had always laughed at his description of Mother's prayers.

But now I enjoyed them. An indescribable feeling engulfed me when we knelt in family prayer. It was indeed like riding the subway, but I've always enjoyed doing that, and now I wished the ride would never end.

1933 (above)
  Back row: Horst, Mother, and Father (Maria and Paul). *Middle row:* Arno, Ursula, and Edith. *Front row:* Karola and Esther.

1936 (right)
  Back row: Arno, Mother, and Father (Maria and Paul). *Middle row:* Edith, Ursula, and Horst. *Front row:* Karola (three years old) and Esther.

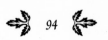

1944 (top)
Left to right: Karola, Mother
(Maria), Ursula, Edith, and Esther.

1949 (middle)
Back row: Edith, Karola, and Esther.
Front row: Father (Paul), Mother
(Maria), and Ursula.

1955 (right)
Paul and Maria Hilbert.

CHAPTER 8

We still hoped for the Western powers to come to Berlin. It would be difficult to be under another country's control but, we felt, at least the Western Allies would be better than the Russians. We dared not let ourselves think about what Russian military control would be like. The way they raped the land and its people made it difficult for us to form good thoughts about them.

Spring of 1945 arrived. The air warmed, and the sun shone for longer periods each day. On the few trees that had been left standing after air raids, buds opened and fresh, pale-green leaves colored tiny parts of our gray, ravaged city: new hope growing out of ashes. Indeed, everyone's hopes seemed to have risen with the temperature. People almost smiled at each other in the streets. Color in our dismal world had a wonderful effect—it seemed to help us forget, at least in part, the wounds that had laid open and fresh during the snows.

Nevertheless, with beauty of spring came the desolation of hopes shattered. On April 20, 1945, the Russian army started its assault on Berlin, penetrating into the suburbs the next day. It seemed ironically clever for them to begin their invasion on Adolph Hitler's birthday. His present from them was the firing of artillery into the streets of our broken city. My beloved

Berlin, scarred with heaps of wreckage where homes once stood, would have to endure another tragedy; but I feared that perhaps this catastrophe could not be overcome.

Ursula, Esther, and I had gone to get some food items with our rationing cards. We were quite a distance from home when the first artillery shells hit a nearby building, raining broken brick and plaster on the street below. My uncomfortably small shoes made it difficult to walk, but when the first blast sounded, I jumped ahead to run!

"Don't!" Esther cried, pulling me back when I leaped into action. "Stay close to the edge of the street. Even the rubble can provide some protection from the artillery."

I looked into her steady yet frightened green eyes and felt her stare dissolve my brief hysteria into a sweaty trepidation. I obediently inched my way behind Ursula along the buildings and rubble lining the street. Esther followed me cautiously. Under my blue blouse, my heart thundered loudly like a band of horses crossing a wooden bridge.

Never had I been in the street when fighting was going on, and never would I want to be there again. The artillery fire made me feel as if I were on the front lines. Oh, how I wished I had a helmet and a trench to crawl into!

Esther must have sensed my panic. She reached for my hand and squeezed it reassuringly. It calmed me somewhat, but I could tell by her moist palms that she was also fearful. We flattened our bodies as small as possible, and inched our way towards home. At times it seemed like we were barely moving at all.

The smell of smoke filled my nostrils; my throat was dry, my hands cold and wet. I felt numb inside, seeing and hearing the artillery fire but not allowing myself comprehension. My movements became mechanical, as if my body knew how to survive without my mind instructing it. I knew that at any moment the pile of ruins we were huddled next to could be hit, shattering the pile into hundreds of pieces of shrapnel that would end everything quickly. If that didn't happen, artillery could hit the building we were inching beside, and shrapnel would pelt mercilessly down on us. Yet I moved slowly, steadily forward as if the scene before me were merely an illusion.

Through the sound of machine-gun fire and cannons booming through the air, I could hear a man's loud, boisterous voice steadily barking out words that I couldn't comprehend. I concentrated on the sound and soon began to understand the words and recognize the voice. It belonged to Joseph Goebbels, Hitler's minister for propaganda and public enlightenment. His voice came from the apartment houses. I realized that everyone must have turned on their radios to try to find out what was going on. The Russians had started their assault on Berlin, and the stations were broadcasting an encouraging speech by Herr Goebbels. The broken windows of the apartment houses didn't provide much privacy. Out of every door and window we inched by came his loud, booming voice announcing, "We are still winning the war! Germany will forever conquer!" If I hadn't been creeping along the outside walls of apartment houses, not daring to move an inch further into the street for fear of being hit by artillery, his convincing tone might have been a tiny bit believable. At the end of his speech he wisely suggested that the people living in the upper apartments take up residence in the basements.

"What fools he must think we are!" I was too angry to laugh at the paradox in his speech. "Everyone knows the end is near. He knows it, too," I loudly hissed.

"Hush! What if someone heard you," Ursula scolded, glaring at me over her shoulder.

"They can't," I retorted. "The shooting's too loud."

When we reached home the house was in disarray. Feather beds, blankets, and pillows had been tossed over the sofa and chairs. Kitchen cupboards were open, a few dishes piled on the table. Half-full grocery nets were draped on the kitchen chairs.

"Mother!" called Ursula, alarm resounding in her voice.

A shuffling sound from the bedroom caught my attention. I had been too engrossed in the mess to notice it before. Ursula and Esther heard it too, and we all hurried in that direction.

"Mother!" Ursula called again.

"Right here," Mother calmly replied, peeking from under the bed. "I'm just getting the rest of your suitcases." Her hair was slightly ruffled, and a few beads of sweat were apparent on her forehead, a sign that this activity was overwhelming her.

"What's happening?" I demanded.

"We're moving to the basement," she told me. "Haven't you heard the shooting?"

"We were in the shooting!" I bellowed.

"Yes," she nodded, compassion showing on her face. "I was afraid for you."

I felt better seeing that I had her sympathy, but apparently there wasn't time for patting heads and wiping tears. She handed me two of the suitcases. "Take these down to our storage area in the basement. Esther, you and Ursula start folding the bedding."

I took the suitcases, stopping in the kitchen to put my grocery net beside the others on the chairs, and started for the basement. It was quite clear that Mother wasn't going to waste another second, and I was glad for her decision to move downstairs. After what had happened on the street, I would have gladly moved into any hole in the ground.

But we weren't moving into a hole, ditch, or trench. In the basement, aside from the large air raid shelter, there were many hallways leading to small storage areas that each apartment used. Ours was about six by twelve feet. I laid the suitcases on the floor of our tiny new habitation and started back up the stairs.

Apparently everyone in the apartment building had listened to Joseph Goebbels's speech. People were running back and forth, bumping into each other in the halls and stairways, unable to see over loads of bedding and food stuffs.

Actually, I imagined it would be quite fun to live in the basement. We would be closer to our neighbors and I loved having people all around me. It gave me a sense of security, I think. I just didn't feel right when not surrounded by people. However, I wasn't looking forward to this Russian takeover. The artillery shots were still arriving in rapid succession. I wondered if we would see the German army at all. It looked to me as if the Russians could walk down our street at any moment and there would be absolutely no resistance.

After moving down bedding, dishes, eating utensils, and anything we thought we might need, Mother called us into the living room. "It's time to go," she said.

After all the hustling around we had done, it seemed strange that the mood we felt suddenly became very solemn, like someone had just been pronounced dead. I watched Mother, not knowing what to expect. Turning to Esther she said, "Play us one last hymn."

Esther soberly walked to the piano and sat down. She played the opening lines to a hymn we all knew well. After the introduction, we all sang, "A Mighty Fortress Is Our God." When we'd finished, we quietly formed a circle and looked into each other's eyes for a moment. I could tell by the looks on my sisters' faces that they felt as I did, uncertain of what was to come. We had each other and I thanked the Lord every day for that, but would that soon change?

When my eyes fell on Mother, however, I felt differently. There was such a power radiating from her. Although her body was weak from hunger and her hair had grayed much more since the war, her eyes revealed her inner self. She had become a mighty spirit, and her strength seemed to bore into me, filling me with hope.

Mother bowed her head for prayer, and we reverently low-ered our heads and put our arms around each other, interlocking them so that we became a tight, unbreakable circle. Mother prayed. All the yearnings of her soul were opened and laid before the Lord. She asked him for our lives, that we would be spared the devastation that surely lay ahead. That somehow we would survive, if that was his will, to raise future generations in righteousness to him. She prayed for our purity, that we would be chaste and no one would steal this from us. That our hearts would be pure and we would not fall into the temptation of working for vengeance or withholding our forgiveness from our predators. That we would share the light and the love of the gospel in whatever circumstances we would be sent. Lastly, she prayed for our possessions and our home. In closing, Mother humbly said, "We ask for these things, kind Father, only if it is thy will. We leave it to thee to decide if we will have or have not. We place all our lives, virtue, and possessions into thy hands: do with them as thou wilt."

After the prayer, we hugged each other while the sound of artillery shots still exploded in the streets. I hoped we would stand there with our arms around each other for a long, long time, but Mother seemed anxious for us to rush down to our new basement home.

"Hurry now, girls!" she cried, breaking our embrace. She eagerly started herding us out of the apartment. We half ran, half walked into the hallway outside our apartment. Mother came last. She swung the front door around but didn't close or lock it. She left it open a tiny bit with a reverent gesture.

I was surprised; if she wanted the Lord to protect our possessions, shouldn't she help him out a little bit?

Edith noticed it too. "Mother, shouldn't you lock the door?" she asked. Esther and I nodded in agreement.

"No girls," Mother began. "We have given everything we have into the hands of the Lord. He will protect it. If the soldiers come and want to enter, they will break the door down. The closed door will not keep them out. If we are preserved and return, we will have no one who can fix the door. I think it best that we leave it up to the Lord, don't you?" she asked with a smile.

I couldn't help smiling back. She thought of things in a different light than I did. During the coming days, when we had to run upstairs for something, we respected her wisdom and always left the door open a crack.

Once Mother sent me upstairs for a better knife to cut the bread, since the one she used had gotten intolerably dull. I went to the window in our bedroom and looked into the street below. I was curious to see if the Russians had reached a road close by so that I could see what they looked like.

I didn't see any Russians, but a German three-wheel vehicle marked with a red cross came driving down the street with a soldier sitting in the back. The driver swerved sharply around rubble, making the vehicle's progress slower than if the occupants had been walking. In fact, it moved so slowly I wondered why they didn't just leave it and run. Especially since they must be in a terrible hurry.

As they came closer, bumping viciously over bits of debris in the street, I realized the reason they didn't. The soldier in the back had no legs! He was desperately holding on, and the rocking movement must have caused him excruciating agony. Even from the fourth story I could see his grimaced face when he turned his head upward in anguish.

Nausea jumped to my throat, and I clapped my hand over my mouth to keep from vomiting. A sharp pain was cutting my diaphragm slowly and deliberately. The room seemed to be spinning, and then a voice cried out, "Oh, why do people have war?!"

The sound was so startling, then the room suddenly stood perfectly still again. I looked around to see who had cried, and realized that it was me. I must have stood by the window for quite some time, because the next thing I knew, someone was calling my name. "I'm here," I answered.

Esther's anxious face peeked at me from behind the door. "What's taking so long?"

"I . . . I . . . I'm sorry," I stammered.

She was by my side in a flash, brushing tears from my cheeks. I hadn't even noticed them.

"What's the matter?" she asked in such a loving tone that I buried my face in her chest and started blurting out the whole story.

Esther smoothed my hair and patted my shoulder as she listened patiently. When I'd finished, she led me to the kitchen tap so I could wash my face. The water was cold. As I splashed it over my tear-stained cheeks, it seemed to wash away my distress.

"Feel better now?" Esther asked.

I nodded.

"Sometimes it really helps to have a good cry," she explained. "I think maybe we try so hard to be brave that we keep our feelings locked up inside until they grow so big they just explode."

I hadn't thought of that before, but I was sure she was right. I wanted to tell her so, but I also didn't want to cut her off.

"I don't know why people have wars any more than you, Karola," she said. "But, I know that it's wrong. It's dreadfully wrong. So many wonderful, innocent people have lost their lives, hopes, and dreams because of this war." She looked intently at me. "But there's one thing that I never want to see happen. I never want to see you lose your hopes and dreams."

I felt ready to cry again as she put her arm around me. "You're my little 'Karl,' and I love you very much."

"I love you too, Esther," I whispered.

We hugged each other a long, long time. Finally Esther broke away. "Come on, we better go. Everyone is hungry, and you've got the knife," she chided with humor. She linked her arm in mine, and we descended the stairs to the basement. Our hair flipped up and down, our skirts swished back and forth, and our free arms swung to the rhythm of our steps.

Suddenly, I felt young, lively, and very happy. I had someone who watched over me, who worried when I was away, and who gave me a shoulder to cry on. Perhaps Esther's wise words would never be quoted by a great philosopher or teacher, but that didn't matter to me. In her own dear way, she had simply said, "I love you—you mean a lot to me." I knew I would always cherish the memory of our times together. I was sure I would forever be Esther's little "Karl." And that knowledge empowered me with rejuvenating joy.

CHAPTER 9

"The Nazi storehouse is opening! The Nazi storehouse is opening!" A young voice carried the cry through the basement and was coming toward our tiny storage area where we had just finished a meager lunch.

Mother, my sisters, and I stared at each other in disbelief. Was the news echoing off the basement walls true, or had our minds imagined the news our hungry stomachs helped create?

"It must be true," I observed. I jumped up from the row of feather beds, which were neatly rolled against the wall and served as chairs in our basement residence. "I'm going to find out what's going on."

Hans, a young boy who lived in our apartment house, was only a few steps away from our narrow entrance door. I stepped out in front of him, forcing him to stop in the cramped hallway.

"What are you shouting about?" I questioned, grabbing his shoulders to help him stop.

"The Nazi storehouse is open!" he called again.

"We heard that," I told him. "What storehouse? Where?"

Mother and my sisters gathered around him, helping him see that we needed more information before he could continue on in delivering the news.

"The white building on Oberbaum Bruecke," Hans

explained. "It's a Nazi storehouse. They're going to open it and let us have the food before the Russians get it."

"What kind of food?" Ursula asked eagerly.

"Who cares," I replied, releasing Hans. "Let's go!"

"But the Russians should be here in half an hour!" Ursula cried, her forehead crinkled with worried lines.

"If there's a chance for food we'd better get it," Mother firmly insisted. She motioned for us to follow her up the basement stairs.

Artillery fire was still pelting down the street, often hitting the sides of buildings and causing shattered brick and mortar to fall like rain. I hardly noticed. All I knew was that we were on our way to find a deliverer from the ravenous hunger that could drive a person mad.

Ahead of us, across the Spree River, I saw the chalky white brick building as one would see a castle filled with wondrous treasure. It rose six stories above us and was fenced in by a high, thick, cement wall. We had been intrigued by that building because German soldiers always guarded the only gate that led into the compound. We saw trucks entering after stopping to show what I had assumed were official papers to the guards, but that was the only activity that went on around that building.

Whenever we had crossed the bridge on the U-Bahn we could see down into the building compound and had decided it was a military domain. We never dared ask about it.

When we arrived at the warehouse, there was complete confusion. The huge crowd that had gathered was riotous. They shoved and shouted at each other, trying to acquire the best place, until it was nearly impossible for the soldiers to open the doors.

The soldiers shoved people away with their rifle butts until they opened the main doors. We were among the many who crowded inside into a dark gray foyer where several heavy metal doors lined the walls. I wondered what lay behind them, and for a fleeting moment my imagination toyed with the idea that this was some sort of trap, and we would all be taken as prisoners by the Russians. In an effort to force that horrible thought from my mind, I concentrated on watching the German soldiers straining against the crowd to open the first door.

Esther and Ursula were standing close in front of me when the heavy iron doors were finally forced open. Inside was a refrigerated storage room filled with all kinds of cheese! The mob of berserk bodies rushed forward and literally carried Esther and Ursula inside.

I watched with my mouth open at the savage selfishness the people displayed, hitting each other, gouging, grabbing food, and screaming in anger or in pain.

After a few minutes, Esther came crawling out with Ursula close behind.

"My glasses fell off!" Esther screamed above the riotous roar. "I bent down and was lucky enough to find them before they were smashed!"

"They're behaving like animals," I declared.

"They're ferocious animals!" Ursula exclaimed breathlessly, coming up beside us.

"Nothing in the world can get me to go back in there," Esther said. Her tone was definite. She threw back her head in scorn as she added, "I don't care how much food they have."

I noticed that her hair was tousled and one of her better skirts, a dark blue one, had been ripped down one side revealing a good portion of her leg above the knee. She looked to where I was staring, and quickly folded the tear over. "Can you believe this?" she cried, pointing to her skirt.

"Meine gute," Mother muttered, covering her hand over her mouth in amazement.

"What could I see to surprise me more?" I angrily interjected, my hands on my hips. I was sure that the people inside would come out looking the way Horst used to look every Saturday after he had fought off a gang of boys determined to make his life miserable because he was a "Mormon" boy.

In spite of the terrible greed displayed by our fellow Berliners, a gnawing question crept back into my mind. "How will we get some of the food?" I asked out loud.

Everyone looked at me, but no one gave an answer.

Finally, Ursula said, "It's suicide to even want to go in there, Karola."

I thought about it. "Yes, but it seems senseless to stay outside empty handed."

A startled cry came from inside, as if everyone had suddenly seen a delightful surprise. We came closer to see it, too. Another room had opened.

People who had practically killed for the cheese in the first room now dropped it all, running for the better. The next room was filled with fresh chicken, sardines, butter, and eggs! Food we hadn't seen in years!

Mother smiled. "Come on, girls," she said. "Cheese is good food."

We each picked up a square of orange or yellow cheese, which I thought must weigh about 40 to 50 pounds, and took it back to our basement apartment. By the time we reached home our arms ached from the strain, but we ignored the pain and ran back for some more. I grabbed a round of cheese this time and started for home.

While I was running across Oberbaum Bruecke, I noticed about five German soldiers who were drilling holes in the center of the Oberbaum Bruecke asphalt. My curiosity grew since we had to cross this bridge to get home. As I watched, I realized that they were filling the holes with sticks of dynamite.

"I'm not crossing that bridge anymore," I spoke to myself.

About halfway home, I found Mother and Ursula going back to the warehouse.

Mother looked worried. The soldiers had just started drilling the holes in the bridge, so I knew that couldn't be what was bothering her. If I could avoid telling her about the dynamite, I would. She looked as though she didn't need any further alarm.

"I haven't seen Esther for a long time," Mother told me when I came to her side. "Not since we were in the first room gathering cheese," she added, frowning thoughtfully.

I tried to think of when I last saw her, and realized I too hadn't seen her since then.

"Karola, will you go and find her?"

Now I knew I must tell Mother about the bridge. "We must find her, Mutter," I said, trying to keep my voice calm. "Soldiers are drilling holes in the bridge. They intend to blow it up."

"Meine gute!" Mother exclaimed, her eyes bulging in horror.

"If she's not over here when the bridge goes, she'll be left on the other side with the . . ." I stopped. Mother knew very well what would happen.

"Don't worry," I said. "I'll go back and find her."

"What about Ursula? She can help, too," said Mother.

I looked at Ursula, and an idea formed in my mind. She was a very pretty girl, which could be useful at a time like this. "Ursula, you can use your charm to get those soldiers not to blow up the bridge until Esther and I come across."

A smile crossed her face. "That I can do," she confidently replied.

"Hurry then, there's no time to waste talking," Mother cried in a frantic tone.

I gave Mother my load of cheese, and she hurried toward home while I ran back to the warehouse.

I searched all over. There were only a few people left looking for food. The mass was gone and the place was starting to look deserted.

The clatter of shots going off outside sharply contrasted with the stillness that was filling the building. It gave me a queer feeling, and goose pimples pricked my skin as my voice echoed through the rooms. "Esther, Esther where are you?" I climbed all six stories and repeated my call, but only an eerie echo came back.

After several minutes I ran back to the bridge to check with Ursula. It occurred to me that I may have missed Esther entirely and she might have crossed the bridge already.

"Has she come yet?" I asked Ursula when I reached the bridge.

She solemnly shook her head. "I haven't seen her, Karola."

I watched the soldiers drilling another hole. "What about the bridge?"

"Oh, they promised to wait for ten more minutes," Ursula said. She was doing an excellent job.

I ran back. Surely I could find Esther in ten minutes, I thought.

"Esther! Esther!" I screamed. There was no reply. I silently prayed as I ran from floor to floor. I couldn't bare the thought that Esther might be left behind, especially since the Russians were so close now.

"Oh, Esther, Esther," I spoke aloud. "You've done so much for me, why can't I help you when you need me!" In desperation, I ran back to the bridge. Ursula saw me coming and ran to meet me.

"Karola," she gasped, out of breath, "Esther still hasn't come. We must pray!"

"Oh, Ursula, I have, I have," I said, a sob catching in my throat. "How long will they give us?" I asked.

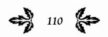

"Just a few more minutes! They have to blow it up!"

"Ursula, what will we do? Esther is nowhere. I called all over that building."

"Take my hand," said Ursula. We turned toward each other, holding hands as Ursula offered a prayer to our Heavenly Father to help us find Esther.

As Ursula opened her eyes at the close of the prayer, she cried, "Look!"

I whirled around and saw—to my great relief—Esther! She was slowly walking towards us as if she didn't have a care in the world.

Ursula and I ran to her, and each of us took her by an arm and hurried her along.

"Thank you for waiting," Ursula called to the soldiers.

"Now you can blow up the bridge—this is our sister," I happily told them as we ran across the bridge with Esther between us.

We hadn't gone very far when a deafening noise burst into the deserted streets, and the ground shook so hard we had to stop running or fall down.

"Where in the world have you been?" Ursula asked Esther when the earth quit trembling.

"What do you mean? I was in the warehouse," she replied, looking somewhat perturbed at the question.

"We've been looking for you for the past twenty minutes," I said. "I didn't see you anywhere in there."

Esther looked thoughtfully at me. "Well, after the awful experience in the cheese room," she explained, "I found a stairway that went downstairs. There were all kinds of dried onions and cabbage and . . ."

"From a warehouse that was full of wonderful things like fresh chickens, you brought dried cabbage?" asked Ursula in mock dismay.

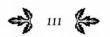

"There was no one down there to fight with and I found some empty sacks. See how much I have," Esther told her defensively while she held open one of her sacks.

I couldn't help bursting into laughter, partly out of relief that Esther was all right, but mostly because the dreadful situation turned out to be so humorous.

"You girls want some butter?" said a voice interrupting my laughter.

We turned to see who it belonged to, and saw German soldiers on a tank with a big barrel full of butter.

"Sure," we said, holding out our hands.

They scooped up some balls of butter and plopped them into our cupped hands. It never occurred to me to check to see if their hands were clean. But I guess ours weren't very clean either. When you can get some food, there's some things that just don't matter.

As we walked into our basement home, Mother was visibly relieved to see Esther with us.

"Goodness, Esther, where were you?" she said, slightly annoyed.

"There was nothing to worry about," Esther said defensively.

"Look in her bags and see if you think there's nothing to worry about," Ursula suggested.

Mother took the bags and stared into them in surprise. We all waited to see her reaction. She threw both hands over her face, her body shaking uncontrollably. I wasn't sure if she was laughing or crying until at last she moved her hands away.

Great heaves of laughter burst out. I hadn't seen Mother laugh like that for a long time. We all joined her, and what made things even funnier was that Esther didn't even smile. She still insisted that there hadn't been anything to worry about; she knew where she had been all along.

In the basement, people gathered from time to time and

started trading. Those who had lots of fresh chickens realized that they would spoil before they could eat them all, so they gladly traded for some cheese. We traded cheese for chickens, eggs, sardines, flour, sugar, noodles, and rice until we had a very good supply of food. Strangely, though, we never traded the dried onions and turnips—I guess because no one ever asked for them.

The Lord had really been good to us. Mother figured that our food supply, if rationed properly, could last us from four to six months.

The pleasure we gained from this knowledge only slightly soothed the anxiety we felt knowing that the Russians were on their way. Blowing up the bridge slowed them down, but it didn't stop them entirely. They constantly fired shots down our street from the other side of the river. It was impossible to cross the street for some air or a visit with a neighbor. You had to creep along the walls of the apartment houses to get outside at all.

One day, Mother, my sisters, and I stood by the apartment house entrance door, which barely hung on one hinge, to get a breath of fresh air. Lunch was over, and we needed a change from being shut away in our little basement city.

I noticed a man in front of the apartment house across the street. He was wearing a strange uniform. It was light brown with a swastika prominently displayed on his left arm. "Isn't that an SA uniform that man has on?" I asked Mother, remembering that the SA were the earliest followers of Hitler.

Her eyes narrowed when she looked at the man. "How in the world does he dare to be seen in that uniform?" she muttered in a low voice.

"I thought the SA soldiers were loyal to Hitler even before he came into power," I said.

"Yes, that's right," Mother nodded. "Now that Hitler has

brought such destruction, how could anyone openly display loyalty to him?"

A man came hurrying down the street, sliding along the buildings. When he reached our apartment house, he stopped in the doorway. He was so disgustingly drunk, I was amazed that he could slide along the buildings without stumbling into the Russians' fire.

He paused right in front of Mother to catch his breath and spotted the man in the SA uniform. The stranger suddenly raised his arm in the Nazi salutation. "Heil Hitler!" he sneered sarcastically.

The SA trooper leaped to cross the street, his fists clinched and his face and ears red with anger, but the Russian shots forced him back. He stormed back and forth. "I'll kill you!" he fiercely screamed.

The stranger moved on unharmed and unruffled. Realizing that he couldn't inflict bodily harm, the SA trooper assaulted our ears with the most offensive language I had ever heard.

"Come girls," Mother said, ushering us away from the door. "We don't have to stand and listen to that."

We spent the afternoon sitting on rolled-up bedding in our basement abode, talking a lot about what might be ahead for us. We didn't worry anymore about the tedious routine of darning, mending, and scrubbing clothes. No one worried about those kinds of things now.

How often I wished that this whole mess would be over and we could go back to living some kind of normal life, like going to school or a movie, or just spending a quiet evening at home. It all seemed so very far away. I knew it had been a part of my life, but it was buried so deep in my memory I had to concentrate hard to imagine things the way they used to be.

"Esther," I whispered that evening as we snuggled under our feather beds, trying to float into a restless sleep.

"Hmmm," she hummed, half-awake.

"Do you think there are still people in the world who go to school or movies?"

There was a long silence while Esther thought. I was just about to repeat my question when she said, "I doubt it, but maybe they do in America."

"Yes, that must be right," I said. In America they probably still did some of those wonderful things. I remembered how long ago Mother wished she had wings to fly to Zion. Now I wished we all could have gone over there where life still held a trace of normality, where we would be far, far away from this place.

CHAPTER 10

On Thursday, April 25, 1945, the first Russian soldiers slowly advanced upon our street. I was puzzled by the fact that we never saw many German soldiers around. Perhaps it was because there had been no actual fighting on our street. Our contact with the German army had been limited to the soldiers we'd seen on the tank, those who had given us some butter, and the ones who had blown up the bridge. Later we learned it was a blessing that we hadn't seen more German soldiers. In the neighborhoods where the Russians and the German soldiers fought, havoc and horror reigned during the confrontation.

The first Russian soldiers to converge on our street were still engaged in serious combat. They rushed into all the basements, pointing guns and shoving people, demanding if anyone knew where German soldiers were hiding.

Just before noon they barged into our basement, knocking things over and kicking obstacles aside as they checked for German soldiers.

"Where are the soldiers?" a Russian asked us as he threw our feather beds across the room. We girls huddled together in a corner, staring at him and wondering what the consequences might be if we didn't have any soldiers for him to capture.

"We have seen some," Mother calmly answered. She had stepped between us and the soldier, the way any mother would stand between danger and her offspring.

The soldier stopped kicking and looked down at her. She seemed fragile and weak against his tall, strong frame, but she stared up into his eyes and said, "We can honestly tell you that the ones we saw left a long time ago."

He grunted a reply and pushed past her out the door. We all sighed audibly, relieved to see that they didn't take anything or hurt anyone.

"Why, Mother," I said, "they're not so bad after all."

Although Mother had appeared calm for our sakes, I knew inside she had been terrified when they stormed in. Her gentle hand was still trembling when we heard the last footsteps die away on the stairs. I hoped I could somehow ease her fear by helping her see they were just men in uniforms. But, as always, Mother saw the situation in a different way.

"Yes," she said, her eyes glistening as she spoke, "and they only asked for German soldiers. Just remember, your brothers are German soldiers! What will they do to them and the many good men and fathers that were drafted into the army?" A tear slipped quickly down her thin, ashen face. "We are now a conquered people," she soberly added.

"Mother, don't you think the soldiers seemed just like every other soldier?" asked Ursula while she straightened her feather bed on the pile with the others.

"People must stretch the truth about them," Edith suggested softly.

"People usually do," Mother acknowledged.

"Let's forget about the soldiers! The worst must be over now!" shouted a voice. I looked up to see Hans, the thirteen-year-old neighbor boy who simply adored Ursula. Lately he kept appearing wherever we were to see what she was doing. He always found a way to involve himself, and Ursula didn't seem to mind his presence.

"What are you talking about?" Ursula asked.

"I know where there is a gramophone and some old records," Hans offered. "Let's listen to some music for a change."

Esther's face lit up at the mention of something musical. "Go get it!"

"I'll be right back," he said, turning swiftly away.

"I'd rather eat," said Edith with a mischievous pout.

Mother smiled at her. "You can help me slice bread and cheese for lunch."

Esther and Ursula went into the hallway to find Hans and start the party. I decided not to miss out on the fun, so I followed them. I felt like a third wheel with Ursula and Esther. They had been spending more and more time together and becoming great friends at that time. We walked through the labyrinth of hallways and found an old table tipped over on the floor.

"Let's set the gramophone on this," Esther suggested.

We had just finished lifting it upright when Hans arrived with the gramophone.

"Oh, where did you find it?" exclaimed Esther, clapping her hands with delight.

Hans blushed slightly as he set the gramophone on our table. "Oh, just around with some old stuff," he told her.

"Wind it up—let's hear some music," Ursula directed.

The gramophone cranked and whirred when Hans gave the arm a few vigorous turns. I laughed. It seemed to be crabbily saying, "I don't want to move—I'm tired!"

Esther blew the dust off of a thick old record and fit it into place on the turntable. At first it hardly sounded like music at all. The record was so scratched I couldn't discern exactly what song it was supposed to be.

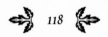

"That doesn't sound too good," Ursula complained.

Hans seemed wounded, as if Ursula had stepped on his stomach. Then his face brightened as he thought of a new idea. "Here, I can fix that; move over!" He brushed Esther aside and carefully placed his finger behind the gramophone's needle. He gently moved it along so that it either skipped over the scratches, or only replayed them once. Now it really sounded like music!

Esther watched the record spin around and around, intent as a hungry wolf watching a rabbit he planned on eating. Ursula tapped her foot in rhythm. Sometimes she would have to hold her foot up a second longer than normal to wait for the gramophone to repeat a beat. Hans cranked the arm and pushed the needle while trying to keep an eye on Ursula.

I smiled with pleasure. The peaceful scene inspired me to feel that the day could turn out to be better than usual. The Russians had passed by without harming anyone, we were listening to music we had almost forgotten, and lunch would soon be ready.

Suddenly I noticed a movement behind Ursula. I'd been so busy watching my sisters I hadn't seen it before. When I realized what it was, I froze.

Esther noticed that I neither spoke nor moved, and turned to see what had caused my temporary paralysis.

A Russian soldier stood behind Ursula and Esther. He was holding a machine gun, and a strange sort of grin curled his lips.

"Let's go back to Mother," Esther softly advised. "She'll know what to do."

We turned and broke into a swift run back to our part of the basement. We hoped the soldier would get lost in one of the winding hallways and be unable to follow us. We paused shortly to catch our breath and look behind us. Hans must have stayed by the gramophone because he hadn't appeared, but to our immense disappointment, the soldier had.

We started off again, dashing quickly around corners until we felt we must have finally lost him. We slowed to a walk and came to the hallway outside of our basement storage area. Mother and Edith were waiting by a barrel, improvised as a table, with some sandwiches.

"We've been waiting for you," Edith told us. "Hurry and sit down so we can pray."

I looked at Ursula and Esther and saw them exchange glances that said, "We won't mention what just happened."

"Say the prayer, Edith," Mother said.

Edith had barely finished when the soldier appeared behind us again.

He studied each one of us very thoroughly, taking in every minute detail of our appearances. A lascivious smile spread on his lips when his eyes fell on Edith.

"Get up," said Mother. "Everyone slowly walk to the main part of the basement. Don't let him see we are afraid of him."

We rose shakily and started walking toward the common area in the basement. Mother was the last to leave, and the soldier followed us closely. We walked as fast as we dared, trying desperately to appear calm. I quickly glanced back at Mother and saw that the soldier was trying to maneuver himself in front of her, next to Edith. His demeanor meant trouble, as if he would use every method at his disposal to get what he wanted.

Ursula and Esther suddenly flew into a frantic run for the main bomb shelter. Edith ran for the courtyard with the soldier and Mother right behind her. I quickly glanced at the main basement where Mother had told me to go. I didn't want to be disobedient, but one thought filled my mind: I had to follow her outside to the courtyard. I stayed close by her because something seemed to order me not to leave.

I had never seen Mother so horrified. Her face was drained of any color. Her eyes were wild with fright. Her fragile frame moved with speed and skill as she ran ahead and then darted back, trying to keep herself between Edith and the soldier.

When the soldier managed to move between them, Mother forced herself in front of Edith again. At last, in frustrated anger, the soldier slammed his machine gun against Mother's chest. A short grunt escaped her, as if the gun had taken her breath away. He made wild angry gestures, babbling in Russian, but we all understood what he meant. If Mother moved again, he would pull the trigger without hesitation.

I was close behind her and gently put my arms around her, hugging her arms tightly to her side in an effort to keep her still. She mustn't, mustn't move. I placed my cheek next to hers. "Please, Lord," I silently begged, "Don't let him shoot my mother!"

Edith watched from a few yards away. Her eyes were large and frightened; she stood immobile in her terror.

An elderly man who lived in our apartment house carefully walked up to the soldier. He tried to speak Polish to him, but the angry Russian threw him to the ground with his free hand. The man scrambled to his feet and stepped out of the crazed Russian's reach.

The soldier glared at Mother and then looked at Edith. He seemed to realize that he couldn't reach her as long as he had to hold the gun on Mother. We were at a dangerous standoff.

In this desperate situation, another soldier came into the courtyard. Black fear poured like tar into my chest as I realized that together they could accomplish their desire. But then I looked at the second soldier's face. His whole countenance shone as if he were a heavenly being and, in that moment, I believed that he was.

He walked with calm majesty to the soldier who held us at gunpoint. I heard him speak gently, in unrushed tones.

We all watched quietly, as if hypnotized by the sound of his voice. As he spoke, I noticed that the soldier's machine gun began to drop. I glanced at Edith and saw that she noticed it too. Slowly, oh so slowly, it fell lower and lower until at last it aimed at the ground.

Simultaneously, we bolted with all our speed for the basement. Ursula and Esther stood in the doorway, apprehension lining their faces.

"Quick, hide!" Mother cried. We all scurried away like frightened rabbits.

The terrible clomp, clomp, clomp sound of many soldiers' boots tromping down the metal stairs hushed the cries of fear around us.

In the rush to find hiding places, Esther and Mother had been separated from us. Edith, Ursula, and I found a small room in one of the hallways. As soon as we entered, I realized it was the basement of the little grocery store that was on the first floor in our apartment house. A ladder-type staircase in the room's darkest corner had a trapdoor at the top that led to the small store.

Edith climbed partway up the stairs. "If they open the door, we can slip out the trapdoor and slide something heavy on the top," she whispered to us. "That would give us time to find a new hiding place in the store."

"If the trapdoor is so heavy they can't open it, they might leave us alone," Ursula whispered back.

My stomach cramped as I heard the soldiers smashing and moving things, trying to find our hiding places. There were angry shouts and startled cries as they moved about. It sounded like the older men were angry about something the soldiers were doing. Then a loud slapping sound hushed the protests.

"No! No!!" a horrified scream filled the air, and I nearly let my own voice join in the terror. I had to clap both hands over my mouth to keep from crying out.

The shrieks for help sounded as if they would tear out the membranes of the young girl's throat. They continued, desperate, pleading, yet hopeless.

When I dared trust my voice to a whisper, I asked, "Edith? Edith?" The fear in my voice made it sound like a whimper. "Is that Esther screaming?"

We listened to the sounds of anguish as the girl begged to be left alone.

"I don't think so," Edith answered doubtfully. It was so difficult to be sure. The voice seemed distorted by the force of the screams. How could we be certain that it wasn't Esther who had fallen victim to the cruelty of the soldiers? Could I dare run help her, fighting with all the strength my feeble body possessed to save the virtue of my sister? Or would I easily be captured and share the same fate? What could I do? They were so many, and they had guns.

I couldn't stand it anymore. I sank to my knees, weeping and praying to the Lord to make them leave her alone.

Her pleas for mercy and the soldiers' sickening laughs blended into the most indescribably appalling sound I have ever heard. How could it be possible for them to smile through the sound of another human being's screams of agony? And yet, they seemed to find some perverted pleasure in it. Truly, every tale of horror we had ever heard about these men appeared to be true.

After the darkest eternity, it was finally over. We heard the soldiers step upstairs against the faint, frightened sobs of the girl they had just defiled.

At last we dared to come out. With great relief, I found that

Mother and Esther were safe, but the violated girl, who we barely recognized as a neighbor, was only thirteen.

"They stole my watch!" a man cried. "They came down the stairs with their arms covered with watches, and yet they stole mine! The vandals!"

I looked at him, wondering why that would matter.

"They took jewelry, cameras, suitcases . . . anything that wasn't nailed to the ground."

"They must have a severe shortage of watches in Russia!" said a neighbor woman.

I frowned at this crude attempt at humor. How could anyone see anything even slightly amusing after what had happened? The thirteen-year-old girl had disappeared; but for me, her cries still filled the room.

People around us were amazed at what the Russians had taken. Some cried out in rage; others fell into shocked silence. As for me, I held a quiet vigil for the unfortunate little girl.

The sound of boots clomping down the stairs drowned out the angry grumbles and, as quickly as it had ended, the nightmare began again.

We ran for our hiding places, and as we passed Mother she cried, "Girls, pray! Pray that we get a little rest so we can think of what to do!"

We didn't know that these soldiers were the relief troops. They had more time on their hands. Their tents had been pitched in the streets, and they were settling in for the night. We cried and prayed constantly for the Lord to deliver us. There was no law, there was no order; no mercy came to our aid. Hell ran free, wild, and laughing all around us.

Although we were in danger of being discovered, I prayed out loud. I simply couldn't hear what I was saying unless it was audible. My prayer engulfed my whole soul until I felt I was doing more than praying, more than just asking my Father for help out of a difficult situation. I was pleading, begging for my life and my virtue, and that of my mother and sisters. All my strength focused on prayer. My struggle was so intense that sweat broke out on my forehead and I felt as weak as if I had struggled to free all the victims of the wicked soldiers myself.

Out of the pit of despair our pleas rose. Past the chaos, the torturers, and the tragedy around us, our cries reached the Master of Heaven and Earth. Our Lord heard our petition. It was enough.

Shortly after 5 P.M., the relief troops took down the tents they had set up in the street and moved two blocks further toward the city center.

As soon as the soldiers moved out, we went back to our basement room. Still shaking and weak from praying so hard, we gathered around Mother, eager to hear any words of comfort or guidance she might have to offer.

"I know what we are going to do," said Mother, her voice was strong and sure.

My sisters and I looked up at her. In the last few hours she had aged visibly, but her eyes revealed the inner strength she had received. As I looked into them, that mighty strength seemed to be sustaining me as well. "Horst said they don't like to climb stairs, so we are going to the attic."

A ray of hope burst through our shattered world. Yes! They wouldn't climb the six stories to the attic! They probably wouldn't even try the second floor. Since they knew that everyone was staying in the basement that's the only place they would likely go.

Besides, anyone would be crazy to live up there with the bombs bursting through the night. There wouldn't be a chance for protection from the bombs. But for me, it would be the closest thing to heaven. I would much prefer a bomb to what that thirteen-year-old girl had just been through.

"We mustn't tell anyone where we will be," Mother explained. "They might talk the soldiers into going up there to find us if they feel they are in danger."

"Will we come down for fresh water?" Edith asked.

"We will tell Hans to bring us fresh water. He can be trusted," Mother replied.

We gathered a few necessities and quietly proceeded out of the basement, across the courtyard, and up the stairs to the attic. The roof was partially destroyed by fire and artillery, and a clear, blue sky stretched above us. We could hear the sounds of 48 and 36 shots coming from the Russian rocket launcher, the Stalin Organ, in the street below. Yet, up here we were far away from the terror and confusion.

It wasn't the grandest place we had ever lived in. The floor was littered with half-burned shingles, broken glass, and beams from the phosphorous bomb that had come through the roof. Still it would provide the greatest gift we needed at the moment: peace.

"Let's have a family prayer," said Mother.

We piled our feather beds, pillows, and suitcases in a corner and brushed a small spot on the floor clear of the rubble. Then we reverently knelt down in a circle.

Mother instructed each one of us, beginning with me, the youngest, to say a prayer and thank Heavenly Father for his protection. At first I struggled for the right words to express my gratitude. I knew we had been greatly protected; it was no accident that the relief troops were ordered further into the city. I knew the Lord had heard our prayers for deliverance. Now I desperately wanted him to hear our prayers of thanks.

As I struggled, I found that words gradually began to flow. I opened my heart, and the message I needed to express lay waiting within. Each of my sisters in their turn gave beautifully heartfelt prayers. I felt the Spirit burning inside me until every tiny cell seemed to be aglow with a flame.

Then it was Mother's turn. If one day I should reach the age when time erases parts of a person's memory, I know this is one part that will remain intact. She prayed as if our Heavenly Father were right there in the attic with us. She told him of our love, our desire to be instruments of service in his hands, and most especially our gratitude for being snatched from the jaws of hell, which seemed to be gaping its mouth open after us.

I didn't dare move or open my eyes when the prayer was over. I feared that if I did, this feeling would be gone—and I wanted to have it with me forever.

My sisters must have felt the same. For the longest time we knelt there in silence, letting the Spirit warm our souls with the love we felt for one another and our Heavenly Father. At last I opened my eyes and started hugging everyone. Sobs caught in our throats, and tears of joy streamed unchecked down our cheeks. Planes flew over us, artillery fired in rapid succession, untold horror reigned below us in the city, but we were safe. The moon and the stars lit the sky. Heaven warmed our hearts, and we slept in the arms of peace.

Hush, hush, girls!" Mother said in a whisper. She sat on a wooden barrel close by the attic door. I didn't think we were being too noisy as we played games and occasionally broke out into laughter, but Mother's fine-tuned ear had become extremely sensitive to extraneous noise. When she warned us to be still, we knew she heard something on the stairway below.

Edith moved closer and knelt at Mother's side, listening intently. Since the incident with the Russian soldier two weeks before, it seemed to me that Edith had become very protective of Mother. She went to Mother's side at the slightest hint of danger, much as a small child would.

The rest of us watched, quiet and wide-eyed, as if to ready ourselves for the worst. The only one who had ever come to the attic was Hans, but Mother was most cautious.

At last she let a pent-up sigh escape. "It's Hans," she said. By then we could all hear his well-known footsteps, so much softer than the clomp of a soldier's boot. We heard a careful thud when he set the water pail down to give his arms a rest.

"Ah, fresh water—I'm thirsty already," Ursula said. She hastened to the door and opened it before Hans could knock.

"Come in!" Ursula offered, making a sweeping gesture with her arm.

Hans's smile was drawn yet happy. His eyes sparkled with the anticipated pleasure of some glad news he had yet to share.

Ursula took the silver ladle and gulped thirstily.

Mother must have noticed the gleam in Hans's eyes, too. "Hans, what is it?" she asked, apprehension clouding the normal tones of her voice. "Have you news of the war?"

Hans smiled broadly.

"Tell us, tell us," I begged, loudly tapping my foot with impatience. "Don't keep us in suspense!"

Hans inhaled deeply and suddenly let his news out with a big bang: "The war is over!"

We all stared at him in disbelief. His blond hair was so dirty that the once lavish curls lay flat against his head. His face was smeared with streaks where he must have wiped sweat with the back of a grimy hand. His clothes were soiled, crumpled, and far too large for his hungry frame. We studied every part of his person and found no clue that he was lying or teasing.

"The war's over!" Hans cried again, twisting his hands, frustrated at the awkward silence that met him.

These words, the words I had dreamed of hearing for so long, finally reached my ears and, strangely, I felt almost as if I couldn't comprehend them. *Could it really be? The shooting and suffering are really over?*

I felt as if I were having a hallucination. *We have lived in a war zone for so long; surely it could never change,* I thought. *This horrible time will just go on and on, never stopping.* Yet I inherently knew that things measured by time must come to an end.

Mother and my sisters must have been struggling with the news as I was. Difficulty comprehending was etched in Edith's brow; Esther stared at Hans with a perplexed look; Ursula stood, mouth agape; and Mother kept shaking her head as if the effort would improve her hearing.

"It's over, I say. I swear! The Germans didn't win, but it's finished at last!" Hans tried once more to convince us of the truth of his news.

We quietly sat down in a circle on nearby barrels and boxes that had become our chairs. Hans stood in the middle and began telling us everything he knew.

"There's even been a Russian commandant stationed just around the corner from us. He's supposed to establish law and order."

I felt a lightness in my chest when I heard this. Surely this represented some measure of safety. The soldiers would be punished for their crimes and we could live safely in our homes even though we would still be under Russian occupation.

Hans finished all his news. "I've got to go back or someone may wonder where I've been. I haven't told anyone about you, although there have been a few wild tales I would have liked to embellish."

"What did they say?" asked Edith, leaping to her feet.

"I'm teasing," Hans told her with a chuckle. "They just noticed you were gone, but no one even asked me if I knew where you were, so I didn't have to lie about it."

"Thank you, Hans," Mother told him with a gentle smile of relief. "We all greatly appreciate what you've done for us."

Hans blushed and dashed out the door.

When he'd gone, I turned back to Mother, whose usual worried demeanor was still evident. Her countenance hadn't changed since the Russians took over the city. The soft gray that had once adorned her head had turned completely white. Worry lines webbed her forehead, and dark circles framed her eyes. She was freakishly thin and could probably frighten any living creature—until they looked into her eyes. The Lord's spirit stilled burned brightly there. But strangely, after hearing the wonderful news, her troubled expression remained.

"My goodness, what's the matter, Mother?" I asked. "We've just heard the news we've longed to hear for six years. Won't it mean that we are going to live a more normal life?"

Mother studied each of us thoughtfully. I knew this meant she was thinking of something the rest of us had overlooked.

"Girls, I am very happy that the war is over," she began. "But you must understand that this doesn't mean things will change overnight. The Russians are still occupying the city, and we don't know how long that will last. If we live or die, it is still in the hands of the Lord." Her voice was thoughtful, as if she were listening to an inner voice of wisdom.

Yes, Mother was right. We shouldn't expect everything to go back to normal very soon. Things had strayed so far from normal it might take years before we could enjoy a life similar to the one we had before the war.

"Do you think we'll be able to move back into our apartment?" I asked hopefully.

"I don't know. I guess what we need to do is find out if we still have anything left there. Maybe there's less in our apartment than we have up here. It might not be safe yet."

"I'll go," I offered.

"No, no," Mother said sternly with eyebrows raised. "I will go and see what's happening in the basement. I wonder if we'll even have any food left down there."

"I doubt it," said Ursula. "Everyone steals from everyone. Ever since people started losing their homes they think that justifies stealing from those who haven't lost everything."

"Gather your things together," Mother instructed. "I'll be back in half an hour."

Mother left, and we took down the clothes we had hung on ropes strung around the attic. We still couldn't wash our clothes—Hans didn't bring enough water for that—but airing them out this way helped to freshen them.

After packing our clothes we started packing the food we brought. We had cheese (of course), hard bread, canned fish, dried onions, and the cabbages that Esther had brought from the Nazi storehouse. We also had dried peas, which we would soak overnight in a little leftover water to soften and eat raw in the morning.

When everything was packed and ready, we sat on our boxes and barrels to wait for Mother.

"Should we play a game while we wait?" I asked.

"I couldn't concentrate. I'm too excited!" Esther replied.

"Me, too. I'd rather just sit and wait," added Edith.

I went to the attic window, which was now just a hole in the wall with a blackened sill on the bottom, and peered down at the street. It looked much the same as it had for the past two weeks. I was too far away to hear any activity in the street. We had considered this a blessing, but now I wished I could hear something, anything that would indicate the Russians would be moving out soon.

I imagined that when the Russians left there would be a great shout of joy that could be heard all the way to America.

"I think we can go back," said Mother breathlessly.

I whirled around to see her just coming through the doorway. She had announced her good news before she even came in.

"Great!" I yelled, throwing both hands into the air.

"Would you girls believe it? Not a single thing has been taken from our food supply in the basement."

"That is truly amazing!" Edith exclaimed, gathering her things in her arms. "I thought for certain that everything would be gone."

"Yes, when our neighbors discovered that we were no longer around, I thought they would take all our food," Ursula said.

"If they didn't, the Russians surely would have," I added.

"Well, that's the amazing thing. It's all there, ready for us to move it back to our apartment. And it is true about the Russian commandant around the corner from our apartment house. He's supposed to have some law restored."

"That's wonderful!" exclaimed Edith.

Mother shook her head sadly. "I'm afraid that he doesn't help much. The people I talked to said that whenever anyone runs to him for help, he denies that a Russian would do such a thing."

We looked at her dumbfounded. Of course he would know that a Russian soldier would do terrible things. How could he sit idly by when exercising his authority could help save property, virtue, or lives? This meant we still had neither law nor protection.

"So things really haven't changed too much," I noted with dismay, sensing the loss of part of my optimistic joy.

"I'm afraid change will come very gradually," Mother told me. "They are talking of a twenty-five year occupation." Then, seeing my despair, she added, "Karola, don't ever think that things will be like they used to. Scars from this war will continue to plague our lives long after the city is rebuilt, and they say it could take fifty years for that."

I nodded that I understood, but I really didn't. I wanted to cry out because of the injustice of it all. If only we could have gone to Zion we could have avoided all of this terrible tragedy. Why didn't the Lord take us there? What good had it done to keep us in war-ravaged Berlin? Unanswered questions kept whirling about to mock me. I just couldn't see why the Lord had let us stay here.

"Come, let's gather our belongings and take them to our apartment. Everyone is moving back out of the basement, and we need to get our things from down there, too," Mother urged us.

I picked up my suitcase and feather bed and followed Mother. I was slightly apprehensive about what we might find in our apartment. After all, we lived in a time of total chaos. People stole from one another as if it were the customary thing to do. Those who had lost everything in the air raids justified their stealing because we were all Germans. We were in this together; if they had nothing, should others be more fortunate? I found it hard to blame them, though. Some people would have to stay in their basements to live until their apartments were rebuilt. All that was on top of them was a huge pile of rubble, nearly as high as the second floor and so wide it blocked off part of the street.

As Mother opened the front door to our apartment, we stood there a moment, slowly breathing in the sight that met our eyes. All was just as we had left it. Not so much as a single needle was stolen.

"Meine gute! My girls, would you believe it!" Mother said triumphantly. "Our Heavenly Father is watching over us constantly."

"It's as if we are living in the hollow of His hand," I reverently said. "How else could we have survived the war so well?"

Mother seemed to be studying me as she stared with her mouth partly open. "Karola, I believe you've put it exactly right."

I dropped my gaze to the floor, somewhat embarrassed by Mother's complimentary observation.

"I can't believe how much you've grown," she said. "And I don't just mean physically."

The day was spent merrily moving back into our own home. We made several trips to the basement for our food and occasionally passed our neighbors doing the same thing. A few people were stationed at doors and windows to whistle if they saw a Russian soldier coming. Mother told us if we heard the whistle to drop everything and run for the attic. Fortunately, we never had to. No warning signal came.

In a way, the whole day reminded me of the day we had moved down and how I thought it would be nice to have our neighbors so close by. But that weak gladness had been slight compared to the way I now felt. Each time I gathered a load of food, my feet raced back up the flights of stairs to our apartment on the fourth story. It was as if the dream would vanish if I stayed away too long.

That night we snuggled deeply inside our own beds. They felt so soft and warm, I didn't want to sleep for fear of missing a moment of this happiness. But too soon I was sleeping soundly.

In my nightmare, the Russians were chasing us. Heavy soldiers' boots clomped after us, and we couldn't move fast enough to stay away. I'd jump in the air and start swimming so they couldn't reach me. I heard a scream and looked down to see that they had caught Edith.

"No!"

I bolted upright in bed. The room was dark and quiet, but a loud banging noise came from downstairs. I heard a woman scream again, and I jumped out of bed and raced to the door.

"What are you doing?" Esther stopped me with her question.

"Someone's screaming!" I told her.

"Yes, the soldiers are breaking into an apartment downstairs."

"But why?"

"To get what they want, Karola," Ursula informed me, somewhat impatiently. "You know that."

"I thought we would be safe here," I said, sliding my feet toward my bed and throwing the covers over me. Somehow it wasn't as comforting as it had been before.

"We'll hurry to the attic if they come up this far," Mother told us from the doorway. I didn't know how long she had been there. "I don't think they will; they'll get what they want from the other apartments," she added sorrowfully.

"Shouldn't we tell the Russian commandant?" I asked, grasping for reassurance.

"Don't you remember? People have tried, but he doesn't do anything," Edith reminded me.

"Go to sleep if you can, girls," Mother told us. "I'll let you know if we need to leave."

I buried my head under the pillow and tried to drown out the noise. My heart cried out for justice for these poor people who had nowhere to turn. They were left to the mercy of their conquerors. But the soldiers had no mercy. They didn't believe in God or God's punishment, only in their own strength to be as ruthless as they pleased.

The lustful troops usually satisfied their carnal whims on the floors below. Or perhaps there was another reason they didn't come up to our apartment on the fourth story. At any rate, we prepared ourselves. We planned a strategy: if anyone came to the door, my sisters and I would hide in one room while Mother began leading them through our place. As soon as she was out of sight, we would rush back up to the attic and wait there for her to come tell us all was well.

Through all this turmoil, strategy, and worry, there was something still to be glad for. At least we didn't have to go out on the streets looking for food just yet. All of the food we had stored filled our little pantry. It seemed miraculous to have food untouched in the basement, simply waiting for us to claim it. I felt somewhat smug and happy not to have to worry about food for a while, but Mother saw it differently.

One day I watched her standing by the pantry door. Her eyes filled with tears of gratitude, then she spoke to the Lord, "Oh, Lord. Thou has given us so much . . ." her lips trembled noticeably. More and more her conversations with God sounded as if he were standing right there beside her. "Surely, there are some of thy people that have need of the food thou hast given us. I can't dare to send the girls out on the streets, but please open a way for us to share it with them."

Half an hour later the doorbell rang. My sisters and I tiptoed to our hiding place while Mother opened the door.

"Sister Hilbert?" asked a kind voice.

"Yes?" we heard Mother answer. There was a short pause before she exclaimed, "Oh, Yes! Brother Garg, do come in!"

He acted as though he hardly recognized Mother when she opened the door. I didn't blame him. When we girls saw that it was Father's first counselor in the branch presidency, we rushed out, eager to greet him.

"Come and sit down," Mother offered.

We settled on the sofa and chairs around him, anxious to talk. I felt so excited to see a member of the Church and a priesthood holder that my stomach turned cartwheels. I put on my very best smile for our company and acted as a young lady should, proper of manner as Mother had taught so well.

"I came to see if you survived the war," he said.

"Dear brother, I am touched by your love for us," said Mother. "Have you been able to reach other members of the branch? What about the ones that live fairly close to you?"

"My good Sister Hilbert, I wish to spare you this sad news." He hung his head as he spoke.

"Please, Brother Garg," Mother urged. "I need to know."

He nodded slowly. "Some of our elderly sisters are starving. I have seen them take what little food they could find from the garbage of others."

"There surely wouldn't be much food in the garbage of hungry people," Edith observed quietly.

"That's true." He raised his head, his moist eyes glistening. "What can be done for them?" he sobbed.

"I'm glad you came, Brother Garg," Mother stated, and her eyes twinkled. "Come here, I have something to show you."

She led him to the pantry and slowly opened the door.

I smiled at his large eyes and open mouth.

"Would you dare take food to those who so desperately need it?" she asked.

"Oh, I can carry food to all!" he exclaimed happily. He looked as if someone had just opened the door to heaven and invited him in.

My sisters and I hurried to the kitchen and helped him fill our grocery nets with food. He tenderly carried the nets to the door, turned, and nodded a "thank you" to Mother. I felt he didn't speak his thanks because he was so overcome he couldn't use his voice.

He returned many times that day and refilled his sacks. I marveled at Mother's faith. She shared what she had at a time when we didn't know if the Russians were going to allow Germans to slowly die of starvation or have ration cards; we didn't know just what would become of us under their control.

Once, while he stood at the pantry loading a sack, Mother asked, "Brother Garg, I've been thinking, shouldn't we have a church meeting to help lift the spirits of the branch members?"

"Sister Hilbert, our branch meeting place has been destroyed. We would have to try to find another place to rent."

"You could hold it in my home," Mother offered. "I could open some canned food and make sandwiches for a nice meal afterwards."

"That would be wonderful!"

"Why don't you tell everyone when you take their food to them?" she suggested.

"Do you want it this Sunday?" he wondered.

Mother licked her lips as she thought. "I think it best to

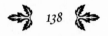

have it as soon as possible," she told him. "These people need the support of one another. Let's not delay."

The following Sunday the first postwar branch meeting was held in our home. Anyone who dared to walk the streets came.

It was good to see the members and sad, too. Everyone showed signs of starvation and loss. It was difficult to be so young and so lively and yet witness the loss that ravaged those around me. These dear ones carried many scars and, try as I wished, I could never go back and relive my childhood in complete happiness.

Prior to the meeting, the wounds of war lay open and bleeding; but as we sang the closing hymn together, I felt a real change had taken place. I looked around at the faces of the branch members and saw that the slow process of healing had begun. In my heart I prayed that the Lord would allow these people to be restored completely.

When the closing prayer was finished, my sisters and I quickly ran to the kitchen to pass out the sandwiches and canned food. I felt a warm tingling in my center as I served each person. I was so glad Mother suggested that we eat afterwards. Each bite that was taken by a hungry mouth brought joy to my soul.

After eating a sandwich, I went to each individual to shake hands. All of them were heroes to me. They had bravely come through untold anguish and despair. A current of love and strength passed from their hands to mine.

"I pray that the Lord will keep you and help you heal," I whispered as I put my arm around an elderly sister beside me, giving her a gentle, loving embrace.

She looked up as if she were thoroughly inspecting me, and said, "You are young, Karola. You will heal completely. The young have a way of putting these things behind them. But when you're old, like me, it haunts you."

I opened my mouth to offer further encouragement, but she patted my cheek and shook her head. "I hope when you are my age these tragedies will leave you alone."

She shuffled slowly towards the door. As I watched her go I wondered if she were right. Mother had never talked about haunting tragedies, only faith in God.

As the elderly sister crept past Mother, I compared the two. Mother was as physically weak and pale as the sister, but her essence was clearly different. She trusted in the Lord with all of her heart and never murmured a word of complaint about the circumstances we lived in. It was as if passing through this tragedy had helped her faith become invincible. Indeed, the war had had a negative effect on her body, but a positive one on her spirit.

"I will pray for you," I softly whispered after the elderly sister as she passed through our front door. "And I will also pray for myself so that when I am your age, I will be just like my mother."

CHAPTER 12

The Allies divided Germany between themselves, with portions of Berlin, the former capital city, going to the Americans, Russians, French, and British. At first the Americans and Russians disputed over whether to make the Spree River or the Landwehr Canal the border between their two sections. We lived between the two and prayed that the Spree River would be the border so that we could be in the American sector of Berlin.

Much to our relief, our prayers were answered and the Spree River was the boundary—we were under American control. We had law and a little order again and dared to go out on the streets. We were very close to the Russian sector but thankful that no terrible noises haunted our rest at night.

However, sleep came slowly and didn't stay long. Although our dreams weren't plagued by screams, they were called on by a villain we were very well acquainted with—hunger.

One night, my stomach growled so noisily I immediately awakened. I hadn't been this famished for a long time. Until now, the food we had gathered from the basement had sustained us well. Even though we couldn't cook our food (the gas lines weren't completely inspected yet), the canned and dried foods had kept hunger from overwhelming us. I was never full and comfortably satisfied, but constant hunger hadn't cursed my every waking moment like it did now. Since Brother Garg had come and we had begun sharing our food with the others, our daily ration had diminished drastically. Now there was almost nothing.

As I entered the kitchen, I noticed that Mother was already in her dark blue dress with the white collar. She was cutting the brown loaf of bread she had bought from the baker in the next apartment house. He had sold it on ration cards, and she couldn't resist. Now that the Western Powers had come into Berlin, we had ration cards again.

I couldn't help licking my lips in anticipation of eating my share of the thick brown slices. Mother finished slicing and wrapped the remainder of the bread in a white linen towel to save it for lunch.

"We'll eat when the others are ready," she said to me, then went back to reading the scriptures she had laid open on the table. I could see by the tired look in her eyes that she had been up for a while. She couldn't sleep as soundly as I did; sometimes I wondered if she prayed all night long.

When all my sisters were dressed, we gathered around the kitchen table and Mother offered our morning prayer and blessing on the food.

I barely said "amen" before lifting my slice of bread and biting out as big a mouthful as I dared. If I bit too big, Mother would scold me for not showing good manners. We were starving, but we didn't have to wolf food down like animals.

I didn't even taste the first bite, but as I was chewing on the second, thinking of butter or even strawberry jam that might add flavor to it, a strange, gritty texture filled my mouth. I chewed more slowly, letting my tongue examine my food to help me guess what was wrong with the bread. It tasted like sawdust and dirt.

I looked at my sisters, and by the looks on their faces I could tell they were suffering from the same gritty mouthfuls of the strange bread.

"I wonder why this bread tastes so awful," Mother said, examining her slice thoroughly. I looked closely at my slice and noticed that indeed there were tiny particles of dirt and what must be sawdust in the bread.

"Mutter, he sold you dirty bread," I cried out indignantly.

Mother shook her head slowly, partly with disgust, but mostly with disbelief.

"Why would he do such a thing?" Ursula demanded.

"Do you suppose he makes bread with dirt so that he can get more loaves?" Esther asked.

No one answered. We all had our own opinions as to why the baker in the next apartment building sold bread with dirt and sawdust in it.

"No wonder it was so readily available," Mother mused.

"I'm not finishing mine—I'm not hungry enough to eat dirt," I said, pushing the bread a safe distance away.

"It's still bread, Karola," Mother told me. "We'll have the rest for lunch like we planned."

"Mutter," I said, trying hard to sound like a distinguished fifteen-year-old, "we've never given others anything so poor. Every time we've shared, it has been our best, whether it was food or clothing. We've even let people sleep in our beds while we slept on the floor."

If Mother knew what I was implying she just ignored it and instead pleasantly commented, "It's been good to share what we had with those less fortunate. The Lord has been very generous with us indeed."

That ended the conversation. In one kind comment Mother erased all lesser thoughts. She picked up her slice and began eating again. Edith obediently followed, as did Ursula and Esther. I looked at Mother, then at my dirt-filled slice of bread and let out a heavy sigh to tell her I was not following her example happily. I forced myself to raise the slice to my lips and bite. I closed my eyes to call up the image of bread and jam, which was needed now more than before, to help blot out the grit sifting between my teeth. The sound of dirt grinding gave me goose flesh and was much more difficult to imagine away. Still, I swallowed and bit again.

Mother finished first and wiped some stray crumbs from the table. I inwardly smiled at the sight. Usually we would lick our fingers and daintily catch every stray crumb in our mouths. Only someone who is full wipes a crumb away. This clearly demonstrated that Mother did not savor every bite of her bread, either.

Instead of leaving the table, she looked around at each of us carefully. I knew she had something important to say, and my vision of bread and jam vanished.

"The time has come when we must leave our apartment and go looking for food," she began.

Dread crept up my skin. We knew this day would be coming soon; there was no escaping it. How else could we get anything to eat? Still, it would be very dangerous, and I wasn't looking forward to hunting for food in suburban factories and small villages outside the city.

"I've been talking to some of the sisters in the branch," Mother was saying. "They say that they've met with good luck at a sugar and flour factory on the outskirts of Berlin."

"But that's in the Russian sector!" Edith gasped.

"Others have done it, and so can we," Mother reiterated firmly.

There was complete silence in the kitchen. The ceiling creaked and the sound seemed as loud as if someone had fallen in the apartment above us.

"Girls," Mother finally broke the silence, "the Lord has watched over us before. He will again."

"Yes, but he's done so much, how can we ask for more protection?" asked Ursula.

"If we don't go, we will starve," Mother said. "We want him to aid us, yes, but he helps those who help themselves. Would you want me to ask him to bring food to our front door every day?" Mother paused. "Of course not!" she said, answering her own question.

Ursula hung her head in silence. No one else said a word, so Mother continued, "Today I want Ursula, Esther, and Karola to ride the streetcar that will take you to Treptow [in eastern Berlin] and beyond."

"Will we buy the food?" I asked.

"Our money is still acceptable, and I have some saved, which brings me to another point. It's all right for you girls to go looking for jobs now, too. You could even check up on schooling and see if you could get enrolled again."

"That's wonderful! Things are getting back to the way they used . . ." I stopped and looked at Mother. "Well, maybe they'll never be the same again, but at least they'll start looking that way," I concluded sheepishly.

"Come on, then," Ursula prodded. "Let's get going."

There weren't any dishes to wash, and the floor was as clean as when our breakfast started. I grabbed a light sweater and we departed toward the streetcar.

Food hunting would be very dangerous. But I knew only too well that hunger pains could motivate us to get into a daily food-hunting routine.

The streetcar came. We boarded and started off on our dreadful journey. We had gone only a few blocks when the streetcar stopped. Some roads were so severely damaged that it would be years before they were repaired. We had to get off the streetcar and walk a mile or two ahead to another streetcar. This one took us as far as it could, and then we switched to another one.

Once while walking, we saw a group of tattered German soldiers being herded down the street by Russian soldiers. The group moved slowly, and I knew it was because they were so undernourished. My eyes smarted as I watched their turtle-like pace shifting sluggishly past us.

Apparently the Russian soldiers were tired of the slow pace, or perhaps they found some distorted pleasure in trying to improve the speed. They beat different prisoners with the butts of their guns as if they were a herd of animals. One man who looked very old, but who must have been young enough to draft, could stand it no longer and collapsed to the ground, unable to go further.

Without thinking, I lunged forward to help him, but Esther grabbed my arm and held me back, shaking her head ever so slightly. Under normal circumstances, I would have helped him up and people would have thought nothing of it. But nothing was normal about postwar occupation.

One Russian soldier stepped forward and beat the fallen man ruthlessly. I couldn't understand what good it would do to keep striking a man who had already fallen. I turned my head, unable to watch, wincing at the sound of each smack delivered by the heartless soldier and the sobbing grunts from the prisoner, whose blood poured red over his grimy gray clothes.

How can we all stand here? Will no one help him? I looked around with pleading eyes. Everyone was watching, but no one dared move. They were all as helpless as I. I pulled my sweater tightly around me and buttoned it as if it could insulate my aching heart from the scene around me.

At last another beaten German soldier, wearing dirty rags, listless and haggard as the others, picked him up and carried him in his arms. The Russian seemed satisfied that he was moving with the rest of the prisoners and not lying in the street anymore.

I watched them go, thinking of how loving the other man had been. He did something that Jesus would have done: he gave himself to another when his own body was beaten and bruised. Then I wondered, *Would he have given of himself so tenderly if it had been before the war?*

"Bitte, bitte," a plea from a frightened young voice interrupted my thoughts.

I turned in time to see a blond, curly-haired boy with freckles and beautiful, clear blue eyes, creeping along with the other prisoners. He was probably a year older than I. A face made for laughter was streaked with heavy tears as he looked at us with pleading eyes.

"Please tell my parents what has happened to me," he begged.

He gave an address, and a man standing nearby wrote it down. The young boy seemed satisfied and nodded a thank you as he crept past. I knew that his sweet message would be the last his parents would ever receive from him. He was on his way to a Russian prison camp where the only road to freedom was death. I stared as he went by, trying hard to look calloused to his situation. I dared not draw unwanted "sympathy" from the Russian soldiers. Yet inside I felt numb. I begged the Lord to help us live another day under these unbearable circumstances.

Suddenly I remembered the time when the war had just started. We were coming out of sacrament meeting, our whole family together. Marching down the street was a group of German soldiers. People laughed and sang, waving handkerchiefs and throwing kisses at them, but Mother cried. Now I understood why.

We returned home empty-handed and empty-hearted.

"Did you find anything?" Mother anxiously asked as we walked through the door.

"You can count our first day at food hunting a complete failure," Ursula brooded. She plopped down on the sofa, disappointed.

"We did find some German prisoners," I began.

"Oh, Karola, Mother doesn't want to hear about them," Ursula scolded.

I stopped talking and unbuttoned my sweater thoughtfully.

"What about them, Karola?" Mother gently asked.

I shrugged my shoulders as I peeled the sweater from my arms. Mother was watching me, and, as I looked into her eyes, I saw that she was worried.

"When I saw them I noticed how different they were from the ones we saw when I was a little girl coming out of church," I explained.

Mother slowly nodded, a look of understanding replacing the one of worry.

"I remembered how you said that when they came home there would be nothing but tears. Oh, Mother, how right you were! It seemed to me that they all had tears in their eyes," I concluded, sadness swelling in my chest.

"It's very sorrowful, but true. I remember the homecomings from the first world war," Mother said, empathizing with me.

No one else spoke as the sorrow of the day seemed to settle over us. We each sat in a daze, our sober thoughts engulfing us.

Finally Esther roused herself. "What's for lunch then?"

"Not that bread!" I instantly protested, suddenly becoming defensive.

"Would you like to know why there's dirt in it?" questioned Mother.

"Did you talk to the baker?" I asked.

"I did," she smiled with a nod. "He said that his goat jumped

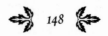

into the dough, but he couldn't afford to throw it away. That's why he sold it so quickly."

"A goat? I absolutely will not eat it!" I screeched, angrily folding my arms across my chest.

"Then you'll have to go hungry," Mother told me matter-of-factly.

She and my sisters sat up to the table and I grabbed a nearby book and buried my nose in it. I kept telling myself that I wasn't hungry and that the sight of them eating goat-dirty bread wasn't tempting me in the slightest. But I knew it was really my pride that kept my stomach empty. I wondered if I would feel less hungry if I swallowed that.

❧ ❧

Although all of Berlin still starved, those living under American control could at least leave our apartments. We didn't have to put ashes on our faces, ruffle our hair into a matted mess, and walk humped over, sometimes adding a limp for good measure. Now we could wear a clean face and combed hair, and walk normally.

The Russian soldiers noticed the change in Berliners, but being across the river, all they could do was observe.

One day while riding the subway, Esther overheard some American soldiers talking about the change in Berlin women.

"The Russians claim that since we came things have changed a lot," said one soldier.

"I'll bet they have," another answered mockingly.

"They say that when they occupied the whole city, 'the German girls were ugly, ugly,'" he bent over and made a grimace to illustrate his point before continuing. "'Then, when the Americans come, they get prettier every day!'"

The soldiers burst out laughing and Esther joined them

without fear. The American soldiers looked at her, and some of them smiled, but they didn't bother her. She even allowed herself to expose a purse she carried.

Esther stepped off the subway at the next stop and hurried off to try to buy food. She had plenty of money with her. Everyone had plenty of money because the German mark printed by Hitler was still the official money. But since food was scarce, the only thing we could really buy with our money was a ticket to foreign movies in whatever movie theaters had survived the bombings.

And we had ration cards. Most of the time you couldn't get anything with the ration card, either. If you were fortunate to get some food, you soon found that it was too small an amount to live on. Somehow, humor survived and we joked, "Rations are not enough to live on and a little more than enough to die on."

Black markets started flourishing. Jewelry, trinkets, tapestries, and other treasures that the Russians hadn't found were cherished prizes. Allied soldiers traded their food for our spoils.

One day Edith came home with some good news. "Karola!" she cried when she came through the door.

"What is it?" I asked, as I put my darning down.

"I've been to the black market and found that the British want German 'Knirps.' They're delighted with them and will pay a good amount of food. Where is yours?"

"But I got it for Christmas!" I whimpered.

"They like the way the umbrella folds down and can fit into purses," she explained.

"I like the way it works, too," I retorted with pride.

"Karola, be reasonable," she pleaded, kneeling down on one knee. "It's worth some food!"

I swallowed hard, looking up into Mother's thin face. My own stomach felt as if it were eating itself.

"It is a treasure," I began, "but food is better. Get it—it's in my dresser drawer."

Edith jumped up triumphantly and dashed to our bedroom for my Knirps. "I'll be back with food!" she said, stuffing it into her purse and rushing through the door at the same time.

I waited through the afternoon to see what my Knirps would bring. I darned socks that had been darned so many times there was none of the original knitting left in them. They did look funny, with different colors of thread making each stocking unique. At least we had some, I consoled myself.

As the afternoon wore on, I grew anxious. I wondered what food a British soldier would give for a valued Knirps. It was useless to avoid thinking about it; constant grumbling from empty stomachs made concentrating on anything but food an impossibility. Day after day I had thought of nothing else but where I could get some food. Now that the possibility for *good* food was present, I couldn't bear the waiting, but wait I must.

I knew that Edith had to go to the British sector at the beautiful gray Brandenburg Gate, which had become a gathering spot for the black market. Once there, she would have to find a British soldier who wanted to bargain for the Knirps. It could take most of the afternoon, if not all.

In the early evening I heard footsteps bounding to our door. I threw my tiresome darning on the arm of a chair and ran to meet Edith.

She burst through the door; a wide smile lit up her face.

"What did you get for the Knirps?" I asked.

She grabbed my hand and nearly skipped with me to the kitchen. "It was a treasure, indeed," she explained, placing her grocery net on the table. "Let me show you." Her eyes sparkled like those of a child who has just received a prized kitten. She slowly opened her bag, allowing the suspense to build.

First came two loaves of bread.

"Bread!" I exclaimed. "Two loaves!"

Edith nodded happily. Next she revealed a pound of butter.

"Oh, Mutter! It's butter, too!"

Edith laughed. "Wait 'till you see what's next."

"I can't wait—hurry!" I cried, miserable with a mixture of joy and anticipation.

"For good measure: a chocolate bar!"

That was more than I could stand. I burst into tears of pure ecstasy. It had been an entire lifetime since I had experienced the thrill of chocolate melting down my tongue and into my greedy throat. This was good eating! I only wished I would have had two Knirpses.

We ate half a loaf of bread with butter for dinner, tasting each delicious bite as if it were angel food cake, or even manna from heaven. When my portion was gone, my stomach bulged as if I had enjoyed a feast, but the best was yet to come.

Edith generously allowed me the honor of dividing the chocolate bar. I cut the pieces evenly and let the others choose first. Then, at long last, I slipped the chocolate into my mouth and let it slowly, slowly melt on my wet tongue. It lasted a good fifteen minutes, and even after the candy was gone, the flavor still filled my mouth with rich, smooth sweetness.

I went to bed grateful that night, and not so hungry. I thought I could still smell the chocolate in the house. My dreams were filled with rivers of chocolate for me to swim in— chocolate houses, flowers, and trees. And, most important of all, no Russians soldiers. Sometimes life could be wonderful!

CHAPTER 13

Edith, Ursula, and Esther went with Mother. It was my turn to stay home and prepare dinner. I didn't like being home alone, but I much preferred it to riding the streetcar into the Russian sector. The vehicle could go only twenty blocks before it had to stop because of the destruction. When it stopped, passengers had to get out and walk to the next available car. At times Russian patrols would be waiting outside the doors and angrily herd everyone into a big group, demanding that all German citizens show their identification cards, which had been issued by the Allies at the beginning of their occupation. We had been given strict orders to carry the cards with us always. And we soon learned why.

As I stood at the kitchen sink, Mother burst through the door. She was in complete panic. "Karola, help me get the girls' identification!" she cried.

"Mutter, what happened?" I asked, alarm piercing my center with a sharp pain.

"The girls were caught in a Russian patrol without their cards," she replied, running to our bedroom. I followed. As I entered our room, my knees locked. I was paralyzed with disbelief. It seemed that Mother had lost her senses. She was flinging our belongings off dresser tops and throwing our clothes out of drawers like a naughty child, a thing completely unnatural for her.

She glanced in my direction and, seeing my open mouth and wide eyes, scolded, "Karola, help me! If I don't get their identifications to them in time, they will have to work in the Red Army kitchen overnight."

"Oh, no!" I gasped, coming to myself again with a jolt. That awful knowledge explained Mother's wild behavior. Working in the Red Army kitchen wasn't what was so dreadful. But what happened after the work was terrible. German girls were not released until the next morning, and, although they were under the protection of the commandant, they were repeatedly raped throughout the night.

"Here they are!" Mother cried and was out the door before I could say another word.

I looked at the disaster around the room and decided it was best to pass the anxious hours ahead by keeping busy. I cleaned and straightened, taking ten times as long as Mother had in scattering it all. That task finished, I fiddled some more with my earlier preparations for a crude dinner. That didn't take long, and I paced the floors until at last Mother and my sisters returned home safely.

"What happened?" I asked the moment the door opened.

"When I came to the commandant's office, I found the girls were next in line to be questioned," Mother began, sinking breathlessly onto the sofa.

"Fortunately they took so many people from the streetcar and took such a long time with each of them that Mother had time to get our identification," Ursula explained.

"When we came before the commandant and showed him our identification, he asked the Russian officers why we had been arrested in the first place," Edith continued, smoothing back her hair.

"They couldn't remember us after all the people they had arrested today, so we were released. We decided not to travel any further to see if there really was food available like there was supposed to be," Esther concluded.

I sank limply into a chair, greatly relieved that none of my sisters had been left overnight to work for the Red Army. "I don't think I'll mind having potato water for dinner," I told them.

"Oh, neither will we," Esther agreed. "Not after today."

"Is it ready then?" Mother asked me.

"It's always ready. Even if it simmers too long, I just add more water," I said. "I only need to put in the potato."

"Go do it then. Grate the potato small and fine," Mother reminded me.

I nodded as I stood up to start grating the potato and setting the table. We had to eat the soup quickly so that we felt like we had actually eaten more than just water, one grated potato, and a few spices. If the soup was allowed to cool before eating, it tasted more like water than anything else.

I finished first and looked at my empty bowl, not daring to wish for more. It would be very ungrateful of me after what had happened. Perhaps tomorrow night I could wish for a piece of hard bread or some peas to put in the soup.

However, neither the next day nor the next brought any improvement to our diet. It seemed only to worsen. The one thing to feast on during that time was good news, which was almost as scarce as food.

Job searching and food hunting seemed to occupy all our time. We spent whole days seeking, praying, risking, finding, losing. We dragged ourselves to factories and farms in every direction. Exhaustion set in long before we could return home in the evening.

One evening when I opened the door to our apartment, I

felt an overwhelming burst of happiness instead of the usual fatigue. Sitting in a chair was a long, thin, tired-looking, middle-aged man. I recognized him at once.

"Father!" I cried, dropping my half-empty bags to the floor and running to his chair. We were expecting him to come home, but it seemed as if he never really would. It was too good to be true!

Painstakingly he stood, and I threw myself into his arms. He laid his cheek on my head and softly patted my shoulder. I buried my face into the front of his wool jacket and didn't bother to stifle my sobs. I didn't realize how terribly I had missed him until I saw him again, sitting in the comfortable old chair that had always been his.

I wanted to bask in the warmth of his embrace forever, but finally I stepped back to have a good look at him. Cracked white lips smiled at me, but the smile didn't cover the haunted look in his eyes. His hair showed new streaks of gray, and worry wrinkles were etched deeper in his forehead. Though his frame had always been tall and thin, his jacket and trousers fit much more loosely than I had ever seen. I tenderly took his bony hand and helped him back into his chair. As he sat down, a painful grimace showed on his face, and I wondered if his suffering were physical or emotional.

I sat at his feet and began my questioning of his activities during his absence.

"Tell me now, Vater," I began. "What was Thuringen like at the end of the war? Did you have anything to eat? Did you miss us terribly?"

Father's gray moustache twitched with annoyance, and I immediately bit my lip. I had asked too many questions, perhaps the wrong ones, and he had become upset.

I looked at him with pleading eyes, hoping he would forget my inquisition. It didn't matter anyway. He was here with us again—we were all together—that was really all I should concern myself with.

As he looked at me, his irritation seemed to dissolve and he quietly told me, "Karola, I prayed for all of you constantly. Not a moment went by when my thoughts weren't turned toward my family, especially when we knew the Russians had taken Berlin. That is all."

I nodded that I understood and gently laid my cheek on his hand, wondering if he was so reserved because he didn't want us to worry or because his experiences left emotional scars that needed time to heal.

An hour passed and I watched the door open three more times, allowing Esther, Ursula, and Edith through. Each of my sisters in their turn ran to Father's side in a state of ecstasy, each told him how they missed him, and each asked the same questions. None of us heard any more about how Father had spent the end of the war.

"Come to dinner now, everyone," Mother called. We quietly rose, feeling the solemn hush that had descended on us. It was as if we were attending a memorial service instead of our own dinner.

At the table, Father offered the blessing. As he spoke, I remembered other prayers he had offered, and I realized this one was very different. Hearing his solitary plea weighed down my soul with sadness. I knew it had been very difficult for Father to leave us alone in Berlin, but at that moment, I realized I would never know of his sufferings because of it.

His prayer ended, and our meager meal began. Half a slice of bread and a slice of boiled cabbage were hardly enough to satisfy my appetite. Father ate slowly but finished quickly. Mother broke her remaining portion in half and quietly placed it on his plate. He didn't seem to notice it was there. Instead he cleared his throat to speak.

"You girls remember when we first came to Berlin?" he asked.

We somberly nodded that we did.

"I had three addresses in my pocket to look at," he said.

"Yes, and you went to the swimming pool and asked the lifeguard where they were," I finished for him.

He continued as if I hadn't said anything. "The lifeguard at the swimming pool told me where to find them, and a voice said, 'Go to Oppelner Strasse.'"

His eyes became moist and his mustache twitched slightly. We quietly waited until he could continue. "I kept those other addresses," he continued at last. "On my way here, I passed those apartments and saw how they survived the war."

He paused again, visibly trying to keep his emotions under control. "They didn't survive at all. They are completely destroyed. If the Lord hadn't directed me to take my family here, we wouldn't have a home anymore."

Father sniffled slightly, and Mother reached over and placed her comforting hand over his. They sat immobile for a long while.

I watched them, thinking so many strange happenings had occurred to them and their family during the war. It was amazing that all of their children were still alive. Now if they could survive the postwar starvation, they would be contented.

Slowly rising, I began gathering dishes, and the stillness in the room gave way to busy sounds of evening chores. The dishes were barely dirty, but I sloshed them in sudsy water and laid them upside down on a towel to drip dry. Edith swept, Ursula wiped the table, and Esther fumbled around helping here and there until she decided it was safe to be excused and lose herself in the chords of the piano.

After the kitchen was cleared and cleaned, we all settled in the cozy living room. I curled up to a book, Edith knitted on a sweater, Ursula mended a dress, Esther played, Mother snoozed, and Father read any leftover newspapers he could find.

I glanced up from my book and absorbed the scene before me. It had been so long since we had enjoyed each other this way. Having Father with us made everything perfect. The priesthood was back in our home and I wasn't so afraid of what might happen tomorrow. I mentally took a picture of that evening to save and cherish for the rest of my life. Too soon, it was time to disrupt our pleasant evening and snuggle our hunger away to bed.

I woke as I did every morning, with a gnawing pain in my stomach—one that grew bigger and couldn't be filled. The agony dragged on and on and on. It was clear that I was slowly starving to death. My family and I were not the only ones in Berlin who felt that way. There were four million people just as hungry. The only thought that occupied every mind was, *Where can I get food?*

We bought food from farmers for whatever price they asked, but we realized it was really begging for food. The farmers didn't need any more money, or anything else. The saying "The farmer's cows have no more room for Persian rugs in the barn" was uncomfortably close to the truth. People couldn't eat gold or diamonds. Food had become the greatest wealth.

❈ ❈

Once Mother and I took the train to Mecklenburg. All of the newer train models had been transferred to Russia, so the Germans used the antique trains. These aged trains had wooden footboards all around the cars and many doors to single compartments with wooden seats. The compartments, however, were reserved for soldiers. The people rode by standing on the wooden foot planks while holding on to rusty side rails. The train resembled a cluster of grapes awkwardly bumping on its way. Mother and I held tightly to the handrail by the window of one of the cars. People pressed us from both sides. It was uncomfortably crowded, but we were traveling.

Although Mother held on as best she could, I knew it was getting too difficult for her to travel this way. I wished I could ease her suffering somehow, but all I could do was hold myself on.

As we bounced along, I noticed that a Russian officer in the compartment by us was staring at me. He was all alone in his comfortable seat, and his stare made me nervous. I started looking at the bombed-out buildings we passed, Mother's tired face, other people, everywhere but in his direction.

At the next stop, someone touched my arm and asked, "Would you like to sit inside?" It was the Russian officer.

I tried to ignore him, but he politely persisted.

"Fraulein, please sit down inside with me."

"You really mean you have extra room?" I stupidly asked as the train began its clumsy start.

"Yes," he smiled. Actually, he seemed quite nice.

I nodded. He turned to enter the compartment, I tapped Mother's shoulder and gave her a gentle push inside.

When he sat down and saw Mother sitting across from him, he was obviously startled. He looked up at me with narrowed eyes. I quickly turned my head to hide my smile.

Mother felt much better after sitting down for a while, and I was glad that I could get the seat for her.

※ ※

Fall of 1945 brought our area some good fortune. Our branch found an old manufacturing building to rent for church

services. We were thankful to have a place to meet again and lucky to find something that hadn't been destroyed.

One Sunday morning when we entered the "meetinghouse," I noticed an American soldier standing off to one side. He seemed very self-conscious and uncomfortable.

"Mother," I whispered, pulling her aside, "there's an American here." I nodded to where he stood.

"He must be a Mormon, too, Karola," Mother answered, and before I could say any more, she was shuffling toward him with one hand outstretched in greeting. I followed closely behind.

"Good morning, brother," Mother cheerfully took his hand.

The American seemed somewhat stunned but quickly replied, "Hello, how are you?"

"I'm so glad you came today," Mother continued, releasing his hand.

The American smiled. "I almost didn't. I didn't know if the people would throw me out."

"Nonsense," Mother scolded. "This is God's church. You are always welcome in his house."

Just then Father came up behind her. "This is an American," Mother said.

Father solemnly shook his hand. "I am Brother Hilbert."

"Call me Brother Scowville," the American offered.

"You speak excellent German," Father told him.

"I was on a mission here in 1939."

"Oh!" Mother exclaimed with delight.

"Yes, there have been many changes here since my mission," he sadly noted.

"I'm sure," Mother nodded. "You must come to our home for dinner and tell us about your mission."

Brother Scowville's eyes clouded. "I can come this evening if that's better for you."

Mother smiled. "Whatever suits you best," she told him.

"I want you to sit with me on the stand so that you can bear your testimony and tell us about Zion. Would you do that, Brother Scowville?" asked Father.

Brother Scowville stood somewhat awed. It took him a moment to gain his composure before he humbly accepted the invitation.

As he and Father walked away, I turned to Mother, "Why doesn't he want to come to dinner?" I asked.

"Because he is a gentleman, Karola. He knows we have nothing for him to eat."

I felt a warm tingle cover me and I thought, *What a kind man he must be.*

During the meeting, Brother Scowville stood and bore his testimony as Father asked. It was so beautiful and humble; the Spirit touched me and the rest of the congregation. Eyes were dabbed and throats cleared almost continually. It was a wonderful experience.

That was the beginning of a lasting friendship. Brother Scowville walked home from our church meeting with us. He never ate with us, but always came in the afternoon after we had eaten. He talked about the gospel and joined us in songs and games.

Each Sunday he stopped by the apartment in the afternoon to walk us to sacrament meeting and came home with us afterward. Mother and Father walked ahead or lagged behind so that Brother Scowville could enjoy the company of my sisters and me.

One Sunday morning, Father gave Esther the key to the main door of our apartment house and explained, "The apartment house is locked before you arrive home."

"It always is Father," Esther said, taking the key hesitantly. "It's a good thing, too. Some of the Russian soldiers have been known to cross the border at night and carry on in the way they're used to."

"Precisely why you girls need the key," Father replied. "I don't like having you arrive home so soon and stand outside the apartment house, waiting for Mother and myself. This way you can come in where it's safer."

Later that day we learned that it was pure inspiration that prompted him to give the key to Esther. After church, as we walked home, three drunken Russian soldiers stopped us about two houses away from our apartment house. One pointed at Brother Scowville and started yelling at him in broken German for not sharing with his friends.

"You are one soldier with four girls; we are three soldiers with no girls. You should share with your friends!"

Brother Scowville whispered under his breath, "Go to the house and stay out of sight!"

We frantically walked away, hearing the complaints of the Russians behind us. We could also hear Brother Scowville trying to appease them.

When we came to the apartment house, we let Esther go first with the key. The key was about five inches long and the keyhole was about an inch long, but even with this obvious advantage, Esther was shaking so terribly that she couldn't insert the key into the hole.

"Hurry, Esther," I urged.

"Schnell, schnell!" Edith cried in exasperation. But our pleas only seemed to annoy her. She dropped the key twice before finally fumbling it into the keyhole.

She turned the lock, and we rushed in. We hurried upstairs to our apartment and to the windows that allowed us to look down to the street.

We heard Brother Scowville below. He was angrily

shouting, "This is the American section and you have no business here!"

We parted the curtain and watched him put the soldiers into their truck and send them on to their own section. He watched them go, then turned and went home in the opposite direction.

As soon as he was out of sight, the truck turned around and came back.

"They're back!" Ursula screamed in a whisper.

"What will we do?" I cried. "They know which apartment house is ours."

"If only we could call an American MP!" Esther wailed.

"What about the attic?" Ursula suggested hopefully.

"They're getting out of the truck!" Edith exclaimed, watching them from the window.

They started staggering toward our apartment house.

"Pray!" Esther exclaimed.

My sisters had bowed their heads and Ursula had just opened her mouth to pray when I sneaked another peak out of the window.

"Look, it's Brother Scowville," I cried with relief. An American jeep with two MPs and Brother Scowville sitting in the back was just rounding the corner.

We saw them escort the three Russian soldiers to the border and wait for them to stay there. We were so relieved and grateful to Brother Scowville for watching out for us. It felt comforting to have such a good American friend.

Then one evening, just as we had finished our meager meal, the doorbell rang.

"Come in," said Father, as he opened the door. "What brings you here during the week?"

Brother Scowville came in carrying a large package. "I just dropped in to say good-bye."

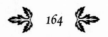

"Good-bye?" I stammered, dropping the broom I held.

"Why?" asked Mother.

"You remember my girlfriend?" Brother Scowville asked as he set his package on the floor by the door.

We all nodded.

"I'm going back to the states to be released from the army. I just got my orders today. Then I'm going to marry my lovely sweetheart."

"How wonderful!" exclaimed Edith.

"We must have a farewell party!" I suggested.

"That's a good idea, Karola. A going-away party for our dear friend, Brother Scowville." Mother added the last with a touch of sadness in her voice.

So Brother Scowville sat with us to play games and sing songs for a wonderful evening tinged with sadness at not knowing if his light would ever shine in our lives again.

After a while, the laughter and songs began to die down, and Mother became serious. "Brother Scowville, I have a favor to ask of you."

He cleared his throat and sat down beside her on the sofa, looking intently at her. "Whatever it is, I will do it gladly," he replied.

Mother smiled. "Thank you," she said. Placing a feeble hand on his shoulder, she continued, "You understand that when Paul and I got married we couldn't get any of our genealogy. The Catholic and Lutheran churches refused to give us any information, even after years of special requests."

"Yes," said Brother Scoville, "I understand."

Mother continued, "When Hitler came into power, we all had to prove we were of Aryan race. The parishes had to give out information. Edith and Ursula did most of the work and gathered our genealogy."

"Wonderful!" exclaimed Brother Scowville, obviously exuberant.

"I know of a sister who emigrated to the United States in the twenties. She does a lot of temple work. If I gave you our genealogy sheets, would you see that this sister gets them?"

"Sister Hilbert, you honor me," he replied, placing his hand over his heart. "I would be happy to do this for you," he said solemnly.

"Thank you so much, Brother Scowville. I'll go get the sheets and her address." He helped her to her feet, and Mother shuffled toward her bedroom.

When she returned, Brother Scowville carefully wrapped the sheets in old newspaper and tied them with a piece of black yarn, setting them by his jacket to be sure not to forget them. Solemnly, as if in slow motion, he straightened and turned to face us. The muscles in his jaw tightened as he struggled to control emotions that threatened to break through his strong guard.

"And now it is time for me to leave," he spoke softly. The moment we had dreaded was here at last.

"I brought you something." Brother Scowville bent down by our genealogy pile, where his army jacket had been carefully placed to hide the bulky brown package he entered with. He brought the box forward, beaming happily at the special secret of what the box contained.

"Please, take it," he told Mother, thrusting it in her arms. I noticed how carefully the package had been wrapped and tied with string. I thought it must be something very special.

Brother Scowville turned to Father and firmly shook his hand.

I couldn't believe he was leaving, and suddenly I thought of a way to delay the inevitable. "We'll walk you to the army bus," I announced.

Brother Scowville smiled at me. "I would like that very much."

"First come tell me good-bye," Mother told him. He rushed to her and threw his arms around her. Tears trickled down Mother's cheek and she whispered, "You have been a very rich friend to some very poor people."

Brother Scowville shook his head. "You are poor in spirit and rich in love, Sister Hilbert. You are a very Christlike people who are easy to be friends with."

Mother smiled and reached for her handkerchief. "You girls go on then," she instructed, shooing us away with a wave of her hand.

We walked quietly, not knowing what to say to this good man whom we might never see again. I found I was glad that no one spoke. It allowed me to feel more deeply the spirit of this man and mark in my mind each moment of our last good-bye.

At the bus stop he shook each one of our hands. "I shall never forget the Hilbert family," he softly whispered. His eyes and nose were red as he spun around to board the bus.

The driver pulled the lever that swung the door closed and then grabbed the gearshift, grinding the gears into first. Other officers and men were noisily talking and smoking, but Brother Scowville stood on the step just inside the bus door, clutching our genealogy papers to his chest, his shoulders hunched over them in a protective manner.

That old familiar feeling of determination, regardless of the consequences, overcame me. I knew I had to say one final thing to him, nevermind who might hear. Throwing caution away as if it were an old mop rag, I loudly bellowed, "We love you, Brother Scowville!"

At first I didn't think he heard me, but after a short pause the choking reply came. "And I will always love you, too!"

The bus lurched forward and growled in protest as the driver threw the gears into second. It picked up speed for two blocks, then turned and vanished out of sight.

At home we all gathered around the brown package with curiosity and began untying strings, passing glances of excitement and anticipation. When we finally got it open, we were speechless. Inside, carefully stacked in rows, were about fifty American candy bars, a luxurious gift indeed.

"My goodness!" Edith finally spoke, breaking the silent spell that had fallen on us.

"Where could he have gotten so much candy?" Esther questioned.

"He must have saved his own candy ration for a long time to be able to give us this gift," Mother declared.

"A very good man indeed," Father quietly pronounced, and we all nodded in agreement.

Weeks later, Mother received a letter in the mail. She opened it eagerly, then smiled as she finished the letter and laid it on the kitchen table.

Mother's smiles were contagious, and I felt my spirits rise as I asked, "Who was that from?"

"Brother Scowville," she replied, placing the letter back in its envelope. He had already found Mother's friend, and the work for our ancestors had begun.

"He deserves a medal for the wonderful way he treated us," I observed. "Those candy bars were better than money."

"The Lord will give him a medal," Mother said. "And the kind he gives is far greater than even the ones the Americans can give. I'm sure that great happiness will always be his."

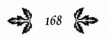

One afternoon in the fall of 1946 when everyone had come home from work, food hunting, and schooling, Mother announced that we had received some good news. "It came in the mail this morning," she said.

"Who's it from?" I eagerly asked.

"Sit down at the table and start your supper," Mother said, taking the yellowing letter from its envelope. "I'll read it to you while you eat."

We quickly obeyed, and after Father instructed Ursula to give the prayer, Mother started:

> My dear family,
>
> I have been released from the POW camp in Northern Italy and sent home to my wife and three children in Leipzig.

"It's from Arno!" I exclaimed happily. "Oh, at last he's home!"

Mother beamed at me. "There's some more":

> I don't know when I will be able to see you face to face again, since, as you know, we are living in Leipzig in East Germany and are not allowed to leave. Perhaps if you find yourselves able, you could make the trip to visit us. Only please, be careful. East Germany is not the same as we once knew.
>
> I love you all,
> Arno

Mother quietly folded the letter and returned it to the envelope.

"Well, he's not a prisoner of war anymore," Father observed, trying to sound cheerful.

"Yes," I quickly agreed. "So many of the prisoners in Russian camps haven't come home at all. We should be very grateful that he was an American prisoner."

"The prisoners in Russian camps come home only if they're dead, or dying," Ursula said bitterly.

"True." Mother slowly nodded her head. "We need to be thankful."

"Then why do I feel so sad?" Esther asked.

"Well, his letter isn't full of coming home to things the way they were," Mother told her. "We all know that so much has changed. At least he's with his family again. Lots of hardships can be borne if one has his family around him."

"Yes," Father agreed. "Listen to your Mother—she understands what she says."

"I only wish we could hear some news from Horst now," I said as I rose from the table. "Then we wouldn't have to worry anymore."

Only a few days later my wish was granted. We had just settled in the living room for a cozy evening when the doorbell rang.

I jumped up and was across the room before Father had even put his newspaper down. Just as I was about to open the door, the doorbell rang two more times and the door flew open.

"Hello!" Horst cried, stepping into the room.

"Horst!" I gasped as happiness swallowed my initial disbelief that it was actually Horst who had burst through the door. I flung my arms around his neck. "Oh Horst, I'm so happy to see you!"

Mother was struggling to get up. Esther and Ursula helped her while Edith embraced Horst next. Father dutifully waited for Mother to take her turn before him.

When we had all finished greeting him and the cries of, "Oh, I'm so happy to see you," had faded away, Horst explained his situation.

"I'm just on my way home. I stopped by only a minute to let you know what happened."

My joy dived to the floor. "You mean you can't stay very long?" I asked.

Horst smiled. "I'm glad to see you mean it when you say you really missed me." He patted my head like he had when I was eight. "I'm sorry, but I have another sweetheart who is worried about me, too."

"Of course," Father affirmed. "You must go on tonight."

"But she's in East Berlin," I objected.

"Yes," Horst nodded. "That is where I live now."

I felt as if a dagger had been thrust into my chest. My dear brother would still be a prisoner, a prisoner of the East.

"Any hardships can be borne if one has his family around him," Mother was saying again. I felt she was repeating her words of wisdom more for my benefit than Horst's.

Horst smiled. "You are so right, Mother." He hugged her once again. "And now I must be off."

I tried to think of something funny to say so that Horst wouldn't feel uncomfortable to see the tears that had started in my eyes. Strangely I remained solemn, as if my emotions were paralyzed. The whole situation didn't have the slightest hint of humor. It was then that I realized what a great gift he had to make people laugh, even during life's most bitter moments.

Horst glanced quickly at me and then looked away. "Good-bye!" he called as he closed the door. I thought there was a slight quiver in his voice, but I wasn't sure. I hoped only that I wasn't the reason it was there, but something told me that I was. He could make me laugh until my lungs begged for air and I was turning blue, but he could never stand unhappy tears. I guess he decided that if you had to die, it was best to die laughing.

"We'll be able to visit him." Esther patted my shoulder reassuringly. "The subway goes two ways. We can go in and out."

"Yes," I nodded, trying to take comfort in what she said. But somehow I still wasn't happy for him. I felt sorrow and a certain uneasiness for the people of East Berlin. I wondered if it were a premonition of what was ahead for them. Would the time ever come that he would enter the East and never be able to return?

CHAPTER 14

"Good morning, Mutter," I cheerfully said one Sabbath morning as I came from my bedroom. In the kitchen, a frail voice cheerily answered, "Good morning."

Mother's attempt to be chipper didn't fool me. She was very sick. Her chalky colored flesh hung loosely on her cheeks, and her eyes no longer sparkled with life and faith. Instead, dark circles framed them, giving her a ghostly appearance. She had become as feeble as a small child. Perhaps being a mother had made her sacrifice more than what was healthy for her. She would eat only part of a meal and begin pushing the rest towards us. Although we urged her to eat her share, she firmly refused.

The worry of finding extra food for us had kept her going, though. It was now up to Mother and me to get food for the family, since my sisters and father had found work. It was a constant, daily struggle that drained Mother's strength entirely.

Branch members helped each other by sharing information about where to find food. In church that Sunday morning, a sister told us of a forest in Mecklenburg County, north of Berlin, where lots of blueberries grew. She suggested that we come with her to pick them since they should be ripe.

We left early Monday morning. Holding to a bar and

resting one foot on a plank, we traveled by train about three or four hours before arriving at our destination.

"There are a lot of ladies here," I said, heading towards the forest with my tin bucket and tub.

"We'll have to spread out," suggested Mother as she followed close behind me.

I moved slightly away from her and started picking. The berries were small and I kept plopping them into my mouth, so it took a long time to fill my tin bucket.

Morning vanished, along with blueberries that stained my hands purple and filled my stomach to the point of sickening me. The autumn sun warmed my neck and shoulders to uncomfortable levels, but still I faithfully plucked berries from the bushes and plopped them into my bucket. At last the container was full. I emptied it into a large tin tub and started the tedious work of filling the pail again.

After picking blueberries for several hours, I was startled by a scream. My blood froze in my veins. "What was that?!" I asked.

The sister in our branch peeked her head out from under a bush and gave me a serious look. "The Russian soldiers know that the blueberries are ripe, too. Be careful."

I understood. Soldiers were a constant terror no matter where you were. I was thankful for the thick blueberry bushes. I knelt down and slid under them to pick that way for a while. The rest of the afternoon, we were plagued by the horrible sound of helpless women first crying for help, then begging for mercy.

"Pray," I heard Mother whisper to me. I knew she was close beside me, although the thick bushes hid her from my view.

I was grateful for the reminder, but this time it wasn't necessary. Since the first awful scream had filled the quiet country atmosphere, I had been asking for the Lord's watchful care.

Night came and we crept under the bushes, smoothing away

twigs and any undergrowth that would jab or poke, making our primitive beds unbearable. We placed our tub and buckets in the thickness of the bushes, fearing that their presence would announce our hideout. At last we tried to settle into sleep.

It was a long night filled with shrill cries, cramped legs, and the smell of ripe blueberries, which by then were repulsive to my stomach.

The next morning we started again, bending, crawling, dragging our tired bodies through the bushes. I felt the ache of muscles I didn't even know I had. I was so terribly miserable that I knew I could never enjoy eating blueberries again. How could I even look at one without vividly remembering those ghastly hours under the blueberry bushes?

At last, evening came and we left to take the last train back home to Berlin. As I shifted my weight from foot to foot and held onto the rails, I uttered a prayer of thankfulness in my heart—not only because we had been able to pick so many berries for our family but also because we hadn't been discovered by the soldiers.

I could see the protection of my Heavenly Father constantly. Of course we were living in a time and place where we needed his constant care. Keeping our lives in tune with the Spirit was essential. We knew if we always remembered the Lord, he would always remember us and spare us.

Mother taught us to have clean hands and a pure heart or our Heavenly Father would not accept us into his kingdom. She said we would honestly do what we could to find food and the Lord would do the rest. We saw many young girls go with American and other soldiers to trade "favors" for food. My parents pointed out that the Lord's commandments had not changed, even if our world had. Immorality had always been, and ever would be, a sin.

Once Mother went with a sister in our branch to the outskirts of Berlin to buy food from the farmers. As they walked through a fresh, green cabbage patch, the sister bent down and picked some cabbage heads, then very quickly put them in her sack.

Mother was shocked. She just stared at the sister, unable to speak.

The sister seemed uncomfortable at Mother's expression, but she shrugged and said, "Oh, well, the farmer won't miss these, but to us it means a lot to have something to eat."

Mother felt troubled but kept silent.

The next week she went alone to the village to see if she could find some food to buy. As she walked through the same cabbage patch, she remembered the other sister. Without thinking, she bent down and picked a head of cabbage.

She wasn't experienced at being dishonest and hadn't looked around to make sure that no one saw her. When she straightened up, she saw a man coming across the patch towards her. Instantly she recognized him as the farmer. To her, it was as if the Lord himself were coming across the patch. Shame swept over her like a blazing blanket. She was stunned! Like fire, the thought burned in her mind—*I expect better things from you!*

Totally humiliated, she held the cabbage head out to the farmer, ready to beg his forgiveness.

He stopped in front of her, drew his hand back, and fiercely slapped her cheek.

The blow knocked Mother several steps back. She raised a hand to cover the sting but said nothing. Her other hand still held out the cabbage for him to take.

She remembered that the farmer stared at her, the anger in his eyes slowly melting away. He seemed touched by her humble, repentant attitude. He took the cabbage from her and dropped it into her sack. Without a word, he reached for her hand and led her to his house.

Mother followed, wondering what he intended to do. Her

fear soon left as she watched him open her sack on the kitchen table and start filling it with all kinds of food.

Later, when Mother told us about the experience, she said, "He muttered constantly that he had never met anyone like me.

"I have begged the Lord for forgiveness all day. In a moment of temptation, I did not withstand. I know how it feels to suffer the Lord's chastisement."

We all stood around the kitchen table looking at her. I couldn't believe that my Mother had succumbed to any temptation. However, it was clear that she had paid dearly.

"Then, do you feel the Lord has forgiven you, Mother?" I asked.

She bowed her head, covering her face with her hands. Her feeble body shook with sobs. Watching her, I wished I hadn't asked. I didn't think my question would bring on such a reaction.

Slowly she raised her head. "He is so merciful," she whispered, wiping her eyes with the backs of her hands. "Yes, he's already forgiven."

❈ ❈

Many of our friends who had emigrated to the United States in the twenties hadn't forgotten us. They, along with former missionaries, would send us care packages. We felt that the Lord had opened the way for us to receive this food so that we wouldn't starve to death. Coffee that was included in the packages was taken to the black market to trade for food.

One of the former missionaries who knew my parents in the late twenties was a dean at Brigham Young University. He didn't know that we had moved to Berlin, and after the war was over and the church tried to send food to Germany, he wanted to get in touch with us. He mailed a letter to our address in

Leipzig. The same mailman was still delivering the mail. He went to an old friend of my parents and asked if she had our address. After eight years she still had it, and the letter was forwarded to us. We received some help from the university dean and felt again that the Lord had opened the way for us.

After Brother Scowville, many American soldiers came to our church meetings. Some of them understood a little German, but most of them did not. We enjoyed the spirit that they brought with them. Our neighbors found it strange to see that the wounds the war had inflicted would not fester in the brotherly love of the gospel. The love of Jesus Christ was truly stronger than anything else.

A group of American soldiers and young women who did secretarial and other work in the army would regularly come to our home on Sunday evenings. We would sing songs and play games with them. They taught us songs like "I Wandered Today to the Hill, Maggie" and "The Little Brown Church."

At the end of the evening, we would stand in a circle and sing the good-night song in German and English and then have a prayer. It was about the only time that we felt young and believed that life just had to get better.

Young love blossomed among our new friends. It seemed to prove that life would again bloom from the ashes that were once our city. A soldier named Joe fell in love with an attractive redhead called Ann. One evening, just as they were getting ready to leave, Joe shyly took Ann's hand and drew her beside him while raising his other hand. "Quiet, everyone!" he called. "Ann and I have something very important to tell you."

Of course, we all guessed what it was. We smiled and nodded at each other as a hush fell over the room.

Joe shuffled his feet in embarrassment. His face and Ann's hair matched in color. "Ann and I have decided to get married."

Cheers filled the room and Joe raised his hand again.

"Brother Stover, the first mission president for the East German Mission, will perform the marriage ceremony."

"Where are you going to have the ceremony?" asked Father.

"There's a little Lutheran church house in Lichterfelde . . ." began Joe.

"They've given us permission to have it there," Ann finished for him.

"And you're all invited!" Joe bellowed, raising Ann's hand with his.

After several heartfelt congratulations, our guests excused themselves and we got ready for bed.

"Isn't that romantic?" Edith questioned with a sigh.

"I wonder what an American wedding is like?" I mused as I unbuttoned my skirt.

"Karola, I can tell that you're not ready for marriage," Edith giggled, pulling her nightgown on. "Who cares what it's like— it's a wedding!"

I sighed with exasperation, taking my pajamas from my top drawer. "I know I'm not ready to get married. I'm not going to get married for a long, long time." I slipped my head and arms into my nightgown and let the flannel slowly slide down to my knees. "I just mean that I've never seen an American wedding. It will be fun to see what the customs are like."

"Quiet," Ursula whispered. "I'm saying my prayers."

I knelt by my bed and did the same before crawling in. But I was too excited to sleep. Thoughts of Joe and Ann's wedding filled my mind.

About a week before the wedding, a rumor spread quickly through all the branches. A new apostle would come to visit Germany and if everything went well, he would get permission to come to Berlin and visit the Saints.

Words can't express the excitement that spread through my whole body. The last apostle we had seen was in 1939, about seven years before. We didn't know what the apostle looked like—we only heard that his name was Ezra Taft Benson.

Despite the lack of telephones, word spread with amazing speed. During the week, someone from the branch informed us that Apostle Benson was in West Germany but hadn't received permission to come to Berlin. He would keep trying.

We prayed that the Lord would open the way for him to come. We so desperately needed to have contact with a spiritual leader and a representative of our church once again.

Then Saturday arrived. We went to the chapel in Lichterfelde for the wedding.

Not surprisingly, we were the first to arrive and had our choice of seats. As we sat down on a bench in the middle of the church, an American soldier entered the chapel. Upon recognizing us, he came over, a smile lighting his eyes with a special secret. "I've just heard the news," he said. "Apostle Benson has gotten permission to come to Berlin after all. The meeting is set for tomorrow."

"Wonderful!" Father exclaimed.

I tried to swallow a lump in my throat as tears of joy swelled in my eyes. *Thank you, Heavenly Father,* I said in my heart.

"Better still," said the soldier, "listen to this. Apostle Benson might even come to the wedding ceremony with President Stover."

I bit my lip to keep it from trembling uncontrollably. To think that we might actually see Apostle Benson today, right here in this very chapel! I was overwhelmed.

My sisters and I held each others' hands, squeezing them from time to time in anticipation.

People were beginning to file into the chapel. We anxiously watched them. They were all soldiers with their girlfriends or people who worked at the American headquarters. No other Mormons were present.

It was nearly time to start the ceremony and still we hungrily watched the entrance. Would he come today? He was so busy that perhaps it was folly even to hope.

Just as we were about to resign ourselves to the fact that he was not coming, a man large in stature with majesty in his step came through the doorway. His hair was slicked back and he wore round wire glasses on his kind, pleasant face. His countenance seemed to radiate with the light of love, and we knew at once that this was Apostle Benson. Our eyes glistened as we smiled knowingly at each other.

We watched his every move. He came slowly down the center aisle, looking straight ahead. The air was filled with his glorious spirit. When he came to our row, he stopped and looked at us. Then a large smile lit his whole face. He nodded to us and walked on.

After all the excitement I had felt about seeing an American wedding, it seemed funny that suddenly the wedding didn't even matter. My only thrill was that I had just seen an apostle of the Lord. I didn't even hear the ceremony.

After the wedding, we left the chapel still somewhat dazed. Major Corbett, who had often come to our home with the soldiers, was standing to one side, and when he saw us, he called us over. I barely saw the major, for standing next to him was Apostle Benson.

"Apostle Benson," Major Corbett said in an enthusiastic voice, "this is the Hilbert family."

"When you come . . . eh, we all know you are Apostle of the Lord," Mother stammered in broken English.

"And when I saw you, I immediately knew that you are members of The Church of Jesus Christ," he replied. "We felt the same spirit."

"Yah," Father affirmed, nodding and smiling vigorously.

Apostle Benson looked at us girls and said, "I have four girls, too, and two sons."

"Our two boys have come back from American prison and live in East, with their families," Mother said, managing a smile. "One is close, in East Berlin," she added quickly.

"They are Mormon boys. You know I love to sing that song 'I Am a Mormon Boy.'"

"Yah, yah," Mother nodded. "We sing this too, only 'I Am a Mormon Child' for girls."

His smile was so enormous it filled my soul. I feared I might explode with joy.

President Stover came up beside Apostle Benson. "The car is waiting this way," he nodded in the direction of Apostle Benson's ride. Apostle Benson shook father's hand and waved good-bye to the rest of us. Then he was gone.

We watched every step he took until, at last, he entered the car and it drove away. I took a handkerchief from my pocket to sniffle into. I was so happy to actually be able to see one of the Brethren again.

The next day in Berlin was a most wonderful meeting. Apostle Benson brought a mighty spirit with him. We felt blessed that the link with the prophet and the headquarters of the Church was truly reestablished after having been broken for so long.

I remembered one afternoon when I was a child and the missionaries were visiting our home. I had lain on Mother's lap, pretending to be asleep, when I had heard her lament, "Oh, that I had wings and could fly to Zion. Our American brethren will leave, and we will have to stay." Now I fully understood what she had meant. We were left behind in a world that had tragically turned from bad to terrible. Even the priesthood holders in our own home were taken away. I wondered why the Lord allowed that to happen. His ways are so mysterious to us. Would I ever understand?

CHAPTER 15

Although the spiritual feast with Apostle Benson fed our souls, our physical hunger remained. We still had a little food coming in from ration cards, but it simply wasn't enough. The responsibility to go food hunting now fell solely on me.

Mother's health deteriorated with the passing of each day. It was impossible to get any medication for her. Her body was weak and sick from starvation. She needed nourishment desperately, but rather than eat all of her portion, she would give some to us. She felt that Father could not work without adequate nutrition, and we girls needed food more than she—my sisters wouldn't be able to concentrate in their work, or Esther in her schooling, on empty stomachs. She felt that I faced treacherous days while looking for food. We attempted to convince her that her sacrifice really wasn't necessary, but all the pleading seemed to be in vain. We simply could not force her to eat more.

One Sunday after church, one of the sisters in our branch pulled me to a quiet corner just inside the front door. By the look on her face, I knew she had a serious reproach in store for me.

"Karola," she whispered in scolding tones, "can't you see

that your mother is dying? She looks thinner every week, if that's possible." She angrily pinched my arm to emphasize her words.

"I know," I nearly sobbed, rubbing the sting from my arm. "We're all pleading with her to eat her share of what little there is, but she just shakes her head and raises her hands for silence. We simply don't have anything to eat."

The fire in her eyes began to die down. "Listen Karola," she said, her voice softening. "There's a certain train that leaves on the Schlesischen Bahnhof in East Berlin at 9 A.M. It goes deep into the Russian occupied zone, far away from Berlin, and stops at an improvised station about two hours later. If you go that far away from Berlin and us poor starving people, you would surely be able to find farms so you can trade or buy food. The train leaves to return to Berlin at 5 P.M. You will have about five and a half hours to search for food, and you'd be back the same day."

A hesitant frown crossed my lips and I looked away from her hopeful eyes.

"Come now," she urged, elbowing my arm, "isn't it worth a try?"

I knew what she was implying: begging for food. At last it had come to that. Somehow I would have to bring myself to do it, for Mother's sake. The thought of taking the train by myself into Russian occupied territory wasn't very reassuring. I despised the thought, but remembering the fragile form of Mother lying on the sofa, wasting away each day, helped me decide what I must do.

The sister waited while I thoughtfully made my decision.

"Well, hopefully, I could get something," I said at last.

She gave me a quick hug. "You're a smart gir. You'll do your best for your poor mother," she reassured me.

I nodded, smiling. "Yes, I'll go and see what I can find."

The next Thursday, I took the 9 A.M. train out of Berlin.

PATRICIA REECE ROPER & KAROLA HILBERT REECE

Standing on the wooden plank, I held on to one of the rusty rail handles outside of a compartment. After two and a half hours, the train stopped at an improvised station, unable to travel farther.

"Looks like the rails have been shipped to Moscow, so this is the end station," declared a short, middle-aged woman behind me. I knew she was trying to impress me by providing this information. I acknowledged her statement with a nod and jumped off the train. I didn't really have time to explain that being from Berlin I knew only too well that anything of even the slightest value was shipped to Russia. Strangely, I had even seen toilets stacked on trucks along with dressers, nightstands, and sofas. The trucks drove away, destination: Moscow.

I looked around at what this particular part of Germany had to offer me. Three oiled roads winding in different directions lay before me. Two of the roads were obviously favored by most everyone who had climbed off the train. I chose the less traveled one, believing I had a better chance of getting food with fewer people to compete with.

I tucked my nets into my backpack and started walking down the third oiled road. I had never been there before, but I thought that this way should also lead to a farm village. I was glad there were only a few other people besides myself on the route.

After walking for about fifteen minutes, I noticed that I was the only one left on the road; others had taken dirt paths that branched off, leading to other destinations.

I stopped for a moment to think things through again. I felt scared and alone. As I looked down the street, I could see by the clump of trees and red rooftops that there was a village about one hour's walking time away.

That was wonderful, until to my horror I noticed the large cluster of buildings between the village and myself. The structures were made from a reddish brown brick and looked like a former German army garrison. I knew that the garrison would now be occupied by Russian soldiers.

I was stunned. We needed food desperately, but I wasn't willing to walk by the garrison at the risk of being raped or murdered. It was too late to return to the end station and try going another way. Everyone would have come to the farms long before I did and I wouldn't have a chance to trade for food. There simply wasn't time for all that and making the evening train, too.

I sat on a tree stump by the roadside to think of a solution. I was thinking so hard I didn't hear the farmer until he was almost next to me. He was driving a broken old cart pulled by a slow gray mule that was flecked with dried mud. The farmer's clothes were as mud-specked as the mule's legs and flank. The smell of manure came from the cart, and I noticed that the straw inside was mixed with clods of the farmer's rich soil. As I watched the wooden cart wobble closer, an idea came to me.

"Excuse me, sir," I yelled, jumping up and waving my arms.

He slowly reined the mule to a halt.

"Would you mind hiding me in that straw?" I asked shyly.

He slowly turned and looked back at his cart, then at me.

I could see a questioning look in his eyes, and I quickly supplied the answer. "I need to get past that Russian garrison. Couldn't you please help me?"

A friendly smile slowly spread across his face. "Why, sure."

I climbed into the cart, and he pulled the smelly straw over me, carefully arranging it to hide every inch of my being.

He clicked his teeth, and the poor, tired mule started forward again.

Nestled deep in my hiding place, I couldn't see anything, but I listened for every sound that sifted through the yellow straw. A door sharply closing and brisk footsteps on cement pavement nearby told me we had reached the awful quarters. I held my breath. I knew the person responsible for the quick steps close by couldn't see me, but I didn't want him to hear my panting, either.

The footsteps faded away, and with them my fear. I waited for the farmer to stop but he continued on. I knew we were nearly at the village and I wondered why he didn't drop me off. I thought I should pop out of my hiding place and ask him, but I realized that there might be some danger I wasn't aware of.

As the creaky wheels stopped, I sat up and looked around. We were just outside the village, close enough for a comfortable walk but far enough away so that no one would see me emerging from the manure-infested straw cart.

"Thank you so much," I said as I climbed out, shaking straw from my hair and dress.

"I understand your plight, Fraulein," he kindly told me. "I'm glad to help."

"Again, thank you," I called as I hurried off toward the village.

I walked to the door of the first house I came to and stood ready to knock. But as I put my knuckles to the door, I realized what I was doing. How could I beg? These farmers didn't really need my money or anything else I had to offer. Everyone tried to trade for food. With all my heart I hated to do this.

A picture of Mother's thin, sickly form came to my mind and with it the courage I needed to go through this new ordeal. I just had to do it for her. Taking a deep breath, I raised my hand to the door and briskly knocked.

A tall woman with a green flowered apron opened the door.

"Could you sell me some food, please?" I asked, pasting a fake smile to my lips.

She studied me thoroughly and after an agonizing moment,

she finally said, "Wait here." A minute later, she returned with a dozen eggs.

I took them and held my money out to her. She shook her head, still scrutinizing me intently, a look of pity on her face.

I was extremely self-conscious and checked myself over to see what she found to be so stunning. With sudden shame, I discovered that the dirty straw had rubbed off on me and I was smelly and filthy.

"At the entrance of the village is a nursery," the woman began telling me as if I'd asked for the information. "They grow all kinds of vegetables for the farmers to plant in their fields. Maybe they will sell some to you."

After thanking her with a slight gracious curtsy, I quickly hurried away. She sadly watched me go. It was then that I realized another thing that must have made her stare: she could see how terribly thin I was. I had never thought before that I was gaunt, yet it was true. I was constantly hungry and weak from lack of nourishment. In spite of the bits of food Mother passed to me, I still wasn't getting enough—none of us had our fill. The kind woman looked well fed in comparison. Her apron even creased into bulges around her waist. As I thought about this, I realized that she must not have seen many people from Berlin. I likely had a good chance of getting food at the nursery.

At the village entrance I found the greenhouse nursery just as she had indicated. I looked around for a while, studying the outlay of the place, deciding whom I should approach and where the supervisor's office might be.

The nursery looked much like a farm, with all kinds of barns and greenhouses made of wood and tin, with glass on top to let the sun shine through. As I scanned the outlay of the place, I noticed a man with a kind-looking face entering one of the smaller buildings. I decided that must be the office, and I followed him.

Inside were neat rows of small vegetables, basking in warmth and light. I approached the man. "Will you sell me some of these plants?" I asked, gesturing towards them.

He didn't look up—he just shook his head. His wide-brimmed hat moved slowly back and forth in the sun shining through the roof. He moved on.

I felt deflated. Without so much as a word it was over. I knew he didn't want to talk to me, but I followed him and tried again. "Please, I have plenty of money."

Again he shook his head. "You have to talk to the owner. Over there in that small wood building is his office."

I went where he pointed and firmly knocked on the already open door.

"Come in," the man behind the scratched wooden desk bellowed without looking up.

"Please may I buy some of these plants?" I boldly asked, although my voice trembled slightly.

He kept his head down as he shook it slowly. He might have had others from Berlin ask for his help; he was not easily moved. Angry that he didn't have the nerve to look me in the eye as he refused to help his fellowman, I became bold. He may not see what I looked like, but he would hear who I was.

"You don't understand," I blurted. "I'm from Berlin. We have nothing to eat. We seldom get anything on ration cards, and it's not enough to sustain us. We are starving to death! My mother lies on our sofa at home, too weak to move." My voice was growing steadily louder, but I didn't care who heard me now. For Mother's sake, I would beg, even from this hardened man. I began shouting. "She refuses to eat food that would keep her alive and instead passes it to us so that we can have more. It's only a little more of nothing!"

At last, he raised his head and looked into my face.

I stepped inside the door, wringing my hands in desperation.

"The rest of my family works for money; I will happily pay any price you ask. Please, sir!" I cried, clutching my hands together in a pleading gesture. "This food is worth very much to me," I continued, a sob catching in my throat. It was critical that I make him understand! "I will pay you well . . ." The despair in my voice faded to a whisper, but I looked at him with pleading, tear-filled eyes that refused to drop until his verdict was announced.

He soberly studied me. I knew I looked and smelled awful after hiding in that dirty straw cart. But I felt I had done my best, and once he made his decision, I wouldn't try again. I had begged to the best of my ability—what more could he want? I knew if his attitude was stony that no amount of begging or money could change his mind.

At last he sighed deeply and nodded. "You may have enough for your sacks," he said. "I'll accept the market price for it, too."

I was jubilant! He took my three nets and filled them up with cabbage, yellow and red kohlrabi, spinach, and even small carrot plants. The carrot green would not be good (they tasted terrible and made your stomach sick), but I didn't say no to any vegetable he stuffed into my nets. I lightheartedly followed him down the rows. It was spring, the ground smelled rich and fertile, the yellow-green plants were the color of a world starting over, food was being placed in my empty sacks, and the day was bright and refreshing.

When the two sacks and backpack were heavily bulging at his feet, I took out my money and handed it to him.

He shoved it in his front pocket without looking at it and lifted the backpack to help me arrange it onto my back.

But I stepped away. I wasn't ready to leave just yet.

He looked up from behind his long-rimmed hat.

I hesitated, summoning all the nerve I had. "If I come again next week, would you sell me some more?" I quickly asked.

A careful smile played around the corners of his mouth. "I guess I can hardly say no now," he joked. Then turning serious he added, "I can see you must be desperate. I'll sell you plants as long as I have them."

My anxiety over his earlier reluctance vaporized into the warmth of the day. "Thank you," I cried, shaking his hand. "I'll try to come every Thursday."

He helped me with my backpack, and I took a net in each hand, nodding a farewell as I turned to leave. I knew he watched me walk away until my form became a tiny dot on the road to the train station. He must have felt very sorry for me.

My heart felt light and carefree due to my good fortune. I knew that once again the Lord had watched over us and provided a way to keep starvation from completely consuming our family. I walked towards the end station on a road lined with tall, green trees. My step was light in spite of my load, the sun was warm, the sky bright blue, and for a time I forgot the suffering I had endured.

The Russian garrison came into view. It loomed by the road like a haunted castle and had the same eerie effect on me. I slowed my pace and looked up and down the road for someone, anyone with something to hide me in so I could get safely past.

Far away down the road, I could hear a vehicle coming. It banged and sputtered along, the engine complaining every inch of the way. When it came into view, I could see that it was an old, forest-green, diesel pickup truck with a rusty hood and cracked windshield. In spite of the appearance of my rescue, a sense of relief spread over me like a warm blanket. Finally, it was close enough for me to wave down like I had the farmer earlier.

I bent to look inside the cab. Kind eyes looked at me from a gruff, unshaven face.

"Please, sir, do you think you could hide me in your truck so that I could pass by that Russian garrison?" I asked.

He glanced up at the compound and a shadow crossed his face. "Certainly," he quickly replied. "Climb in and crouch beneath the dashboard."

I swiftly did as he instructed and he carefully placed my sacks next to me on the seat to obstruct the view of any curious glances we might encounter.

He took me past the dreaded place and as far down the road as he could. When the truck stopped, I opened the door and stepped out. "Thank you very much."

"Anytime," he replied. "I'm glad to see that you had some luck today." He smiled at my bulging bags.

Nodding, I returned his smile before he drove away. With his help in giving me a ride, I was able to catch the train home in plenty of time. The bags seemed light as I leaped off the train in Berlin. I walked briskly under my load. I could hardly wait to reach our apartment and show my anxious family what good fortune I'd had.

I burst through the door and took in the scene at a glance. They were all home, gathered in the front room, trying to keep busy so their hunger wouldn't annoy them while they held dinner for me. "I'm glad you delayed dinner!" I shouted. "Look at what we can have with it." I set my bags on the floor in the front room and opened them, revealing the contents.

They all stared in disbelief at the red and yellow cabbage, kohlrabi, and spinach.

"Karola, how fortunate!" Esther exclaimed from the piano, after rediscovering how to speak.

"Did you have any trouble getting it?" Mother asked from where she lay on the sofa. She carefully scrutinized me as I prepared my answer. I knew I mustn't tell her about the Russian garrison or she would never permit me to return. So I simply explained that I found a nursery that would sell me some food. "They said I could come back every Thursday and fill my bags," I cheerfully added.

"You were most successful," Father solemnly proclaimed. "Between our rations and the food you gather, we should *all* be able to get enough to eat." He placed a special emphasis on the word *all*.

"Yes," I said, going to Mother and kneeling by her side, "that's true, isn't it? You will eat better now, won't you, Mother?"

Mother sighed, "I will eat whatever I can."

"Good!" I exclaimed, jumping to my feet. "With all of this food, there will be plenty for all. You will be looking better soon. Especially if you have these fresh young vegetables as a regular diet."

She smiled at my enthusiasm. "Well, let's stop talking about them and start eating them."

"Do you want me to cook them?" I asked.

"Oh, no." Mother shook her head fiercely. "They're much better-tasting raw."

"Better for you, too," added Father.

I took my nets to the sink and rinsed off a handful of the vegetables. Placing them in a bowl, I hurried back to the table. Father and Edith helped Mother get up from the couch, and we gathered to our places at the table. We blessed the food and began eating. The vegetables tasted so delicious. I thoroughly chewed every bite, savoring the flavor. It was the most magnificent dinner we had enjoyed in a terribly long time.

Every Thursday I followed the same route to the nursery. The owner was very good about letting me buy the plants. Sometimes I actually thought I could see a sparkle in his eyes when he saw I had arrived safely again. I began to wonder if he looked forward to Thursdays as much as I did.

And there always seemed to be a truck driver, farmer's wagon, or cart with a kind man willing to help me pass the garrison unnoticed. Once we passed and came close to the village, I would rush to the greenhouses, fill my nets and backpack with the vegetable seedlings, and return to the road to go back. This way I had plenty of time to find a ride past the garrison.

One Thursday, I left early as usual after loading my fill and paying. I walked as close as I dared to the garrison, keeping myself in the shadows of the trees. I waited and waited and waited, but nothing appeared in either direction. I strained to hear the sputtering of a truck or the awkward thumps of a cart, but I heard only birds chirping and the distant laughter of small children playing in the fields.

I was beginning to get nervous. If I had to walk, I knew I should begin soon. The train would leave in about an hour and a half. An hour would be just enough time for me to walk to the station. I knew I couldn't stay here at night. There was only road, trees, and fields around the garrison. Any Russian soldier could find me during the night, and I would have no protection.

If I didn't catch that train and arrive home as usual, I knew Mother would perish with anxiety. Knowing that I was in the Russian zone all night would be too much for her frail form to handle. If I didn't make it safely home that night she would be dead by morning. This thought caused sweat to break out on my forehead. Hugging a tree for safety and comfort, I anxiously looked up and down the road again.

My agony increased as I saw the iron gates of the garrison open and a large crowd of Russian soldiers file into the street. Apparently they had some sort of break or recess to relax, smoke, and talk. From where I waited, I could even smell the smoke and hear the talk peppered with sudden bursts of laughter. There was no possible way that I could pass by them without being seen. If I were discovered, I could never survive what would be in store for me.

There was no earthly help for me to plead for. No one was coming to my aid. So I turned to the only One who could give me the heavenly help I so crucially needed. Creeping between two trees by the side of the road, I quietly laid my nets down, folded my arms, and closed my eyes in prayer.

I knew I urgently needed the courage to face the most savage enemies I'd ever known so that I could save the life of my mother. She was the one person on earth whose faith had sustained me and given me hope, courage, and a faith of my own at a time when all seemed lost. It was critical that I get home to her.

That day I did more than pray. I begged the Lord for his divine intervention. I felt like I was truly wrestling with the Lord. As I used every ounce of energy I possessed to reach my Father in Heaven, I became deaf to the soldiers' voices and the world around me. My only focus was my Eternal Father.

The instant I began my prayer, I knew with all my soul that He was listening. He was right beside me, hearing each breath I took as I said, "I believe all the miracles Thou has done in the time recorded in the Bible. I also believe all Thou hast done for the people in the chosen land of America as recorded in the Book of Mormon. I know Thou art the same today, yesterday, and forever." I remembered Mother telling me how the Lord had protected Joseph Smith so that he was invisible to the eyes of his enemies. My soul had always been touched by the truth of that beloved story. With fervent conviction, I continued, "Dear Heavenly Father, I know Thou canst protect me. Please make me invisible to the eyes of those Russian soldiers so that I may walk through them unharmed, even as Thou hast done for Thy prophet, Joseph Smith. Help me reach the train so that Mother will not have cause to worry beyond the strength she has to endure."

After closing my prayer, I immediately picked up my sacks and, without a doubt in my heart, walked straight toward the Russian soldiers.

I had to literally plough my way through them. As I pushed one soldier with my right shoulder to have a pathway through, he turned and said something to the soldier on my left. I looked into his eyes and he looked right through me, his big, clear, blue eyes holding no image of me. I continued on my way unscathed. They never even knew I was there.

I caught the train home.

My next dilemma was trying to decide if I should tell my parents what had happened. I knew they had a right to know, especially about how the Lord protected me, but I was still concerned about worrying them.

That evening, Mother and Father retired to their bedroom early. A moment later I knocked on their door and quickly slipped in to talk to them.

They listened without interrupting until I finished each captivating detail of what had happened to me that day. After a long pause, Mother said, "Karola, you have made a tremendous sacrifice to get this food for us. I feel that the Lord has given you this test. You had a sufficient amount of faith to pass it."

"The Lord will not require your sacrifice anymore, and neither will we. Don't go again," Father said with finality. "The Lord will provide. He will open the way for us to get food from some other source."

As he said these words, a feeling of peace came over me, and I knew it was true. I would not be asked to sacrifice that way again. The Lord now knew that I would do anything he required of me for my parents' sake. I knew that now, too. Somehow the door would be opened for us to obtain the food we needed to survive. I gratefully kissed them both good-night and left them to sleep.

Perhaps it was the strain of the situation I had just come through, or the warmth of the peace that now engulfed me; either way I felt tired and wanted to rest in solitude now. I snuggled into my own covers, still somewhat awed by my recent experience. As I thanked the Lord with fervor for the miracle he had provided, I was relieved to know my sacrifice was no longer needed. I would never have to go back there again, and I never did.

CHAPTER 16

There was very little food to eat again. Dear Mother sickened, and there seemed to be no way to help her. My insides felt as if they were being severed when I saw her struggle to the sofa each morning. She would dress and go through the pretense of eating breakfast, then shuffle to the sofa to lie down. She was very brave and never complained, but her body had become so weak she was barely able to move. As she lay, she would softly close her eyes as if the chore of keeping them open was too much for her. She seemed to be waiting. It was clear to all of us that death was merely days away.

Watching her agonize without a murmur was torture for me. I had done all that I could. I couldn't force feed her, and her uncompromising will refused to let her body yield to the necessity of food. It seemed she was allowing herself to die for us, and I couldn't bare it.

How could I stay in the apartment and see the end come? I decided to try to find work, hoping that perhaps the task would take my mind far from home and what was happening there. If all went well, perhaps I could even attend night school to complete my education. I had waited a long time to be able to do this, and now there was nothing more standing in my way.

Each morning my heavy heart closed the door on Mother's

soon-to-be tomb. As I dragged myself away, wondering and praying about what could be done, peace would slowly fill my heart. I remembered again her words: "If we live or have to die, it is up to the Lord." Perhaps it was His will that she go this way. What a crown of glory must await someone who suffers such an agonizing death for their loved ones. This was my Mother—stubbornly righteous to the final breath.

As I began looking for work, I found it was fortunate that I had some experience as an office apprentice. I decided I wanted to be a bookkeeper and accountant. Numbers and figures had never been a problem for me, and I really enjoyed mathematics. It gave me deep satisfaction to organize numbers into rows and find a neat sum. Although some people find that tedious work, I relished it.

Some of the members in our branch told me a lot about business when I first showed an interest. I loved to listen to them and found some of the advice they gave was very reliable.

After looking for a job one morning, I returned home for lunch and to check on Mother. When I opened the door, I was surprised to see several boxes on the table and Mother humming to herself while she cut a slice of bread.

Mother looked up at me. "Oh, Karola, this is for you. I thought you would be home soon."

"Mother, where in the world did you get this?" I asked, walking slowly forward as if in a dream. The smell of food was tempting me, but I wanted her to have the first slice. "Did you have some?"

She nodded and I reached for the bread. After a quick gulp, I repeated my question, "Where did you get it?"

Mother smoothed her gray hair away from her face with the back of her hand. "Sit down, Karola. I will tell you the whole story while you eat."

I obediently sat and slowly savored each bite of the thickly sliced dark bread.

"This morning after everyone left, I knelt by the side of the bed to pray. I had hardly begun when I broke down and cried to the Lord. I explained our pitiful circumstances. I have been surviving on faith and prayers for so long I knew it couldn't last, and this morning it was clear to me that the end was near. It hurt me to envision your life and the lives of the rest of the family if I should pass away," she declared.

"I must have wrestled with the Lord for half an hour or more. When I finished, a great calm came over me, and I knew that help was coming. I lay down on the couch to rest and wait.

"I could hear the main door to the apartment house open and close all morning. Each time someone entered, I would think, *This is not for me*. Then the door opened and someone started up the stair. 'This is for me,' I said, struggling to get up from the sofa. I dragged myself to the door and opened it a few seconds after the doorbell rang.

"There stood an American major. He merely said, 'Wait right there,' in his awkward German. I heard him run downstairs, and a few minutes later, he returned carrying several boxes.

"I was so astonished I couldn't move. He slipped past me and put the boxes on the table.

"'These boxes I brought are filled with food for you and your family,' he announced reverently.

"I couldn't believe it! After I regained my composure, I asked him to sit down and tell me how he knew that we needed this food so badly.

"He said that as he went past the PX store this morning, he felt as if someone pushed him inside. He took a cart and began to fill it with food."

"We could never have gotten that food, Mother. You know

it's only available to Americans," I said.

"Yes," Mother nodded smiling. "Now listen to this. He knew he didn't need anything, so he asked the Lord what he was supposed to do with it all. A deep impression came to him as he remembered the four young girls he had seen in church last Sunday. He had barely spoken to you girls, so he had no idea where we lived."

"How did he find out?" I wondered, swallowing the last bite of my slice of bread.

"He went to the mission home and got the address and brought the food directly here. I told him what happened to me this morning . . ." Mother's voice halted and I waited for her to regain control.

"He said, 'Sister Hilbert, from now on you need not worry about food, anymore.'"

My heart jumped with such force that I was suddenly standing on my feet. Not only had the Lord answered our prayers in providing food, but he had shown me personally that he *would* open the way when my sacrifice was no longer necessary.

I hurried to Mother's side and hugged her frail little body close to me, unable to stop tears that were rushing down my face and wetting my chin and neck. I swam in relief. "He's answered our prayers, Mother. He's answered them again," I whispered repeatedly.

Mother gently patted my head the way she used to do when I was a small child. "Why, yes, Karola. The Lord always answers our prayers," she assured me confidently.

I pulled away to look at her. The moisture from my tears had fogged my glasses. I quickly snatched them from my face and wiped them clean on the hem of my untucked blouse. I put them back on and studied her expression as I tucked my blouse back into my skirt. Her eyes revealed that she fervently believed the Lord always answers prayers.

"But why did he wait so long?" I asked, flipping my brown curls with annoyance. "I don't understand."

"Sometimes he waits so that we will know how much we want what we ask for. Sometimes he waits because the time is not yet right, sometimes to test our faith, sometimes he waits for reasons only known to him, and sometimes the answer is 'no.'"

She was right, of course—Mother always seemed to be. She often said that the Lord moves in mysterious ways, and his ways are not ours. The answer had taken longer than I would have liked, but Mother hadn't doubted.

"You know, Mother," I thoughtfully mused, slicing another piece of bread. "This time the Lord has even provided a way for food to be delivered to our door." I searched her face for a reaction.

Her chin was slightly quivering.

"Do you suppose there was no other way?" I asked. When she remained quiet, I prompted, "Well?"

"Karola," Mother's voice was whisper soft, "I know that he answers prayers in his own way, according to our faith."

"But I never thought he would have food delivered to our front door," I said, pointing to the door to add emphasis.

"Neither did I." Mother walked slowly, painfully past me to her bedroom. At the doorway she paused and, without looking back, said, "Wrap the bread in a towel for supper. I'm going to rest until the others come home." She continued shuffling into her room and softly closed the door.

I did as she asked me to, but I knew she hadn't gone in there just to rest. Even now, I could hear her softly voicing her gratitude to the Lord. I knew she could easily fill the time between now and when the rest of the family came home with fervent prayers. Mother was known to pray all night long.

From that time on, the American major brought food to our

door every week. We even met his wife, son, and daughter. We soon became very close friends.

When the major saw that Mother needed more than food, he started bringing medicine for her. Food and medicine, which had been available only to the American servicemen, were provided for us by the Lord through the good American major. He took care of us, just as if we were his family; indeed, we had become a second family to him.

❊ ❊

During an evening in 1948 we turned on the radio to hear any new developments about the postwar occupation. Sadly, the news that we had most dreaded hit us like wartime bombs.

We sat motionless, barely able to breathe. I firmly closed the book I was reading on my fingers until they hurt painfully. The moment had come; I couldn't escape. I could hope only that somehow we had misunderstood or the announcer had made a serious mistake.

Then suddenly, the message came again. "I repeat, the Russians have cut all access roads and waterways to West Berlin. We are completely isolated. The city is under siege. No supplies will get through."

I felt the hair on the back of my neck stand erect, and a grisly churning started in my stomach. I felt trapped, like a prisoner in a cell with no chance to escape.

"We are a doomed people," said Father as he solemnly sat in his chair, staring at the radio. "We are all going to die of starvation."

Ursula wailed hopelessly. Edith sobbed pitifully, burying her face in a handkerchief, and Esther shook her head and moaned repeatedly. "There's no hope, there's no hope."

Cramps painfully seized my stomach, my palms began to

sweat, and I kept rubbing them on my light blue cotton skirt. Panic was quickly engulfing me, and none of my family could do anything to help.

"What about the Americans?" Mother optimistically asked. We all turned blank stares to her. "They won't forsake us," she insisted.

"Do they care?" asked Ursula doubtfully.

"Let's find out—turn up the radio," Mother told me. "Maybe we'll hear what the Americans plan to do about this."

A tiny ray of hope burst into my prison cell. I flew to the big "Telefunken" radio on our modest wood stand, and turned it up as Mother had instructed. I knelt down beside it, hanging on each word the announcer spoke, desperate for news of the smallest chance that the Americans would rescue us. We all waited breathlessly as the announcer again repeated his statement of doom and the new calamity that had fallen over West Berlin. Anxious minutes passed, and then the announcement came, "The Americans have stated that they will begin an airlift into Berlin. Food and supplies will be flown in. Ladies and gentlemen, the Americans have come to our aid."

"Hoorah!" I shouted, jumping up exuberantly. "The Americans have come to our aid!" I mimicked the announcer. I was so relieved I ran straight to Esther and pulled her up jubilantly. We danced and skipped around the room. I was eighteen, and she twenty, but neither one of us cared if we were acting like children.

And indeed it was true. An American airplane landed and took off from Berlin Tempelhof every 90 seconds. Everything the city needed to survive on was flown in.

I took our grocery nets to the store, opened the door and stopped, staring in complete awe. There it was—cans of fish liver in oil; dried vegetables such as peas, beans, and potatoes; flour, rice, and oats; and sugar! Later there was even canned milk, peaches, and vegetables—food we hadn't seen since before the war, sitting on the shelves where it belonged! I couldn't stop sniffling as I gratefully placed the items on my shopping list into my nets. I heard other customers clear their throats, blow their noses, and sob with joy. What a wonderful blessing it is to buy food from a store!

After loading our nets, I put them on the counter for the clerk to total. It was an indescribable thrill for me to reach into my purse, take out money, and hand it to the clerk! Such an ordinary gesture in common times, but then I felt as if I were living in a new world.

I nearly danced all the way home, smiling and nodding to people, and they smiled back. It felt so good to be young, alive, and well fed! Nothing could possibly cloud my days with misery again, could it?

✻ ✻

It had been only a few weeks since the American airlift began. Our quiet evening at home was interrupted by someone ringing the doorbell. I sighed as I slowly trudged to the door. None of us liked to have our quiet evenings intruded upon. Somehow when the doorbell rang in the evening, we could expect bad news or trouble.

It was the major. A certain sadness clouded his eyes, and the mood in our home was instantly altered.

"Come, sit down," Mother politely offered.

He entered and sat on the sofa.

At first, our conversation was courteous, about things that really don't matter. It reminded me of the type of discussion you would have with a distant relative that you saw only once or twice in a lifetime, not one you would have with a man who had become a part of your family.

As the major conversed, it was clear that he hadn't come to discuss the unimportant things we now spoke of. I could see that something was troubling him. The sadness in his eyes was still prevalent, and he sat humped over as if an invisible weight had been placed on his back. I felt sympathetic and wished he would turn the conversation to the purpose he had come for and unload his burden.

At last a stillness fell over the room and the major bowed his head as if dreading the inevitable. In a quiet voice he announced, "I have come to say good-bye. I have received my transfer papers to Wiesbaden in West Germany."

We were startled. No one moved or said a word, and the steady tick of the clock seemed to slow to an abnormal pace. He was leaving. We'd instinctively known that the day would come. It was only a short time ago that his wife and children had been sent back to America because of his wife's health problems. Now it was his turn to say good-bye, and there was nothing we could do to change that. But how could we let our dear friend and brother leave? None of us doubted that he had saved Mother's life, and perhaps some of ours as well.

"Let's have a song, Esther," I whispered.

The major and the rest of my family looked at me as if I had just told them I was going to jump out of the window. I turned to the major. "We always try to have a merry party when we must say good-bye to our loved ones. In a way, it's what our brother Horst does. That way, they leave with a happy song in their hearts and not sad tears."

A smile finally curved the corners of the major's mouth. "That sounds like an idea that would come from a Hilbert," he said.

Esther sat down at the piano and we all gathered around to sing. Mother was able to stand up for a few of our favorite songs. We sang songs that made us laugh, songs that made us want to cry, and songs that filled our hearts till the Spirit burned within us.

Finally, the time arrived for the major to leave. I felt a familiar sting in my heart as I realized the scene we had witnessed with Brother Scowville was soon to be repeated. It seemed our dear friends would always be leaving to Zion in America and we might never see them again.

Father slipped into his bedroom while we awkwardly tried to prolong the time before we had to say good-bye. Again we spoke of silly things that didn't even matter—anything to postpone the inevitable parting.

"Major," Father said, coming back into the living room.

The major did such an abrupt, sharp, about-face, I thought he might salute him, but he only looked at Father, waiting to hear what he had to say.

"I made a special present for you," he said as he turned one of his most beautiful paintings over for all to see: an enchanting Bavarian countryside, complete with different varieties of evergreen trees, a clear blue stream, and splendid green pastures with cattle grazing in the distance.

"Brother Hilbert, what a beautiful painting!" exclaimed the major, his eyes twinkling with gratitude.

"I painted it for you so that you could remember us better when you go away. I knew the time would soon be here, but I didn't think it would be this soon."

"What can we do to show our appreciation to you?" asked Mother, stepping toward him. "You have helped us so very much."

The major seemed stunned. His mouth dropped open in surprise. We all watched him, searching for any sign that would assist us in discovering what had caused this strange reaction.

"But it was the Lord who paid me much more than what I have done in helping you," he said.

Mother opened her mouth to say something, but he continued, "Let me explain. You see, Sister Hilbert, I came from Zion. The cruelty of war had almost influenced me to lose my testimony. Through you, I have regained it again."

"But, Major . . . ," Mother began.

"I don't want thanks. Neither do I wish for you to mention my poor name to anyone. Let this be between us."

Mother was extremely touched. "Major, your name will always be printed in our hearts, but we will honor your request." She took a step back and seemed to be examining him in awe. "Such a humble man, words can never express how thankful I am to have known you."

"Thank you," the major said, bowing slightly. "You honor me."

The room grew quiet, as if a spell had fallen over everyone in it. It was as if each secretly hoped to freeze this time for us.

A sudden thought occurred to me, and I had to break the silence. "Will we ever see you again?" I asked the major.

He studied me thoughtfully, and then a broad smile crossed his lips. "Certainly, one day in Zion."

I felt my mouth drop open in surprise. "America? Oh, no, Major. If the Lord had wanted us to go to America, he would have opened the way before the war."

"You think?" the major asked doubtfully.

"Yes, it's been Mother's lifelong wish to go to Zion. If he hasn't led her there yet, I don't think he intends on having her go there ever."

The major nodded out of respect for my conclusion. But his eyes spoke of his debate. I was compelled to challenge him, "Don't you think so?"

"Well," he began, "from what I understand, Zion is where the pure in heart dwell. You must remember, I come from the Rocky Mountains, but my testimony wasn't strong enough to withstand the trials of war. I nearly lost the battle until I met this wonderful family. Now, I believe that Zion is more than a place on a map—it truly is where Christlike people live."

"So you're saying that the Lord has already brought us to Zion?" I was astounded by this thought that was coming through the clouds in my mind.

"Yes, maybe a different physical place, but your hearts have been purified. If you had gone to America prior to the war, this may never have happened. Think, Karola, how many people's lives have been changed by your family? I've never seen a home that always had room and food for everyone. Your home has been a haven for the weary. Isn't this what Zion is all about?"

My heart was on fire and I knew the major was right. But there was one thing that was still puzzling to me. It had troubled me since the war began. "But in America there was much more safety then we had here. We could have easily been killed at anytime."

Mother stepped forward to speak, and the major took her hand as if to say, "I know the answer for this hard question, too." He turned to me and said, "You were not alone. Didn't the Lord watch over and protect you? You were still held in his hands, even if you weren't in America. I can't imagine that the Lord would let this precious Zion be destroyed."

I couldn't speak. I felt a warm sensation flowing through my whole being. It was true! We had been constantly protected on our "journey" to Zion—Zion *was* our home!

"Maybe someday you will come to the Rocky Mountains, too!" he added. "Who knows what the Lord has in store for you?"

"Karola, you are only eighteen," Father told me. "Your whole life is in front of you, not behind you."

"Just remember to always live it so that Zion is where you are," Mother added.

"We'll see you again," the major smiled as he patted my arm. "I know it. In every Christlike person we meet, we'll see the faces of the Hilbert family. We shall always find those we share His pure love with in Zion."

Mother stepped beside the major and hugged his strong arm to her frail frame. "God be with you," she whispered.

He was obviously touched deeply as he stroked her hair and finished the words to the song "Until we meet again."

AFTERWORD

At the close of World War II, Germany was divided between the Americans, Russians, British, and French. Eastern Germany fell to the Russians. Berlin itself, which was in the Russian Zone, was divided into four sectors: West Berlin came under American, British, and French rule, while East Berlin was occupied by the Russians. In 1949, the American, British, and French zones formed the Federal Republic of Germany (West Germany), and the Soviet Union established the German Democratic Republic (East Germany). Although the city of Berlin was surrounded by Soviet-ruled territory, the city remained divided between Western and Eastern rule. The Hilbert family missed being in the Russian sector of Berlin by only a few blocks.

Between the summer of 1945 and August of 1961, travel throughout and between the sectors of Berlin was relatively simple, though in the years that immediately followed the war travelling into any Russian-occupied territory was quite dangerous for the German people. As life got back to normal and the Germans began to rebuild, many East Berliners traveled daily to West Berlin for fresh fruit, afternoon movies, entertainment, and recreational visits. The Democratic West was an escape for those who lived in Communist East Germany. Over the years, thousands of political refugees moved into West Germany. Then, on the night of August 12–13, 1961, East German soldiers laid down more than thirty miles of barbed wire through the heart of Berlin. Eventually, the entire city of East Berlin was surrounded by a concrete wall that stood until 1989.

Again, the Hilbert family was blessed; not one member of the family was trapped behind the Iron Curtain. Following is a brief update about each member of Karola Hilbert's family:

Arno Hilbert returned to his wife and three children in Leipzig, Germany, after being released from an American POW camp at the end of the war. In 1952, he was accused of influencing several young men not to join the new East German military. He overheard a Communist committee at his place of employment making plans to arrest him and take him to prison that very night. Arno immediately boarded a train for West Berlin, along with his wife and children. They each crossed the border separately to avoid suspicion and arrived safely at his parents' apartment. The West German government recognized him as a political refugee and flew him to safety in West Germany. He lived in Rheinland until his death in February 1999.

After **Horst Hilbert** briefly visited his family in the fall of 1944 (see pages 73–77), he spent three more days running from the Russian Army. He made it to the West, where he surrendered to an American officer and was placed in a British POW camp. After the war, he was released and returned to East Berlin to join his wife, Irene. They lived in the portion of Berlin occupied by the Russians, and in 1952, he was approached by the Communists to join the East German military. He told them in no uncertain terms how he felt about serving in any military and followed Arno's lead by escaping with his wife and two children to West Berlin. He, too, was recognized as a political refugee and flown to West Germany. He immigrated to the

United States with his wife and children in 1955 and settled in Mesa, Arizona, where he lived until his death in September 1999.

Edith Hilbert married Gert Saltmann in August 1955. They had two children. Edith and her husband owned and operated several bakeries and konditorei shops (pastry shops or confectioneries) throughout West Berlin. They still live in Berlin.

Ursula Hilbert served a mission for the Church in Germany from 1953 to 1954. After her mission, Ursula and Karola asked President Walter Stover, the first post-war American mission president in Berlin, to sponsor their immigration to the United States. He agreed, and the two immigrated in April 1956. Ursula married John A. Wendel of Bountiful, Utah, in the Salt Lake Temple in December 1956. They had three children. John passed away in 1996, and Ursula still resides in Bountiful.

Esther Hilbert followed her musical dreams and became an opera singer in Berlin for the Deutsche Staats Oper Berlin. She married Guenther Adriano Piechottka in 1956. In 1958, Esther was diagnosed with stomach cancer. She collapsed at the opera house while performing in *Madame Butterfly*. She died in August 1958.

Karola Hilbert, whose story this is, immigrated to America with Ursula in 1956. One year later, the girls brought their parents to the United States. Karola married William Lewis Reece Jr. in November 1960 in Ely, Nevada. They were sealed in the Salt Lake Temple in 1971. They had seven children. William died in July 1979, and Karola raised her children alone in the coming years. She served a mission to North Carolina from 1991 to 1992. She now works in the Manti Utah Temple.

Paul and Maria Hilbert immigrated to the United States in 1957 and were sealed in the Salt Lake Temple in May 1957. Ursula, Karola, and Heinz (a son who died in infancy) were also sealed to their parents at that time. Horst was later sealed to them in the Mesa Arizona Temple. After their deaths, Esther and Arno were also sealed to their parents. Maria was diagnosed with cancer in 1960 and died in 1962. Paul lived for nine more years under Ursula and Karola's care. Although Brother Hilbert couldn't understand English, he faithfully attended all of his church meetings until his death in May 1971.